It is said that a Chinese devil will go miles out of its way to avoid meeting one of these stone "watch-dogs." This guardian and its mate protect a Buddhist temple on the sacred island of Pu-to-shan.

Beyond Shanghai

By
HAROLD SPEAKMAN

With eight illustrations in
full color from paintings by
THE AUTHOR

THE ABINGDON PRESS
NEW YORK   CINCINNATI

Copyright, 1922, by
HAROLD SPEAKMAN

Printed in the United States of America.

TO
MY FRIEND
CHARLES E. BUSHNELL

CONTENTS

The Houseboat

CHAPTER	PAGE
I.	15
II.	33
III.	48

River Cities

IV.	73
V.	89
VI.	109

The Island of Buddha

VII.	127
VIII.	144

The Little House

IX.	161
X.	179

ILLUSTRATIONS

"It Is Said That—"	Frontispiece
	FACING PAGE
On the Grand Canal	26
Island Tea-House	46
Chinese Night	66
Mine Host	102
The Cricket Fight	128
Shadow Patterns	140
The Blind	172

To a Chinese Coolie

If those grim artisans in other lands
  Who fret and shirk,
Dropping their chosen tools from listless hands,
  Could see you work

Watching you toil twelve thund'ring hours a day
  In hold or pit
At work which makes most other work seem play
  Compared with it

Giving your body with a man-sized will
  To every deed,
Doing each baneful task as though to fill
  Your spirit's need

If they could hear that constant, cheery song
  Heartbreaking, as it rings
Triumphant to the bitterness and wrong
  Of human things—

Why then, God knows they must look up again
  To a far height,
Stand to their work, and battle on like men,
  Toward light.

Soochow, China.

PREFACE

NAMES of persons and places—when they have any meaning at all—always have an insistent way of calling up pictures before me. For the most part, that works out very well. Mr. Pickwick, Chicago, Agamemnon, Judas, Othello, William Blake, Waterloo, Diana Mallory—these names and a million more embrace the subjects they represent so perfectly that they have become an intimate part of them. But there are others which certainly do not function as they should.

Fafner, for example, the name of the dragon in "Siegfried," *sounds* like the proprietor of a delicatessen shop. Inversely, a small, wrinkled Sicilian who brings three tiny logs of wood (it used to be five logs) for a quarter to my room of a winter's morning is yclept Marcus J. Aurelius. . . . The somewhat astonishing title, Sir Jamshed Jeejeboy, does not belong to the high comedian of a comic opera. Sir Jamshed Jeejeboy himself is a venerable and dignified citizen of Bombay. . . . The tribal name "Satsuma" carried with it only a peaceful picture of kimono-clad inhabitants of the Land of the Rising Sun tranquilly engaged in making their beautiful porcelains—until I came upon a mound near Kyoto under which lie the pickled ears and noses of thirty-five thousand former enemies of the clan of Satsuma!

And—China! *There* is a name to conjure with! What sort of a picture does China bring up? I, for one, had always thought of the Chinese as being a strange, grotesque people. (The years have builded such a vast, irrational barrier of trivial affairs, like chopsticks and queues!) *Dah Sing, Quong Wong, Soo Chow* —there seemed to be something in their very names that made one think of phœnixes, cockatrices, griffins, and other infringements against the spirit of normalcy as we know it. True, the Chinese I had met at different places in the Occident had always been uniformly courteous and friendly. Yet I always had the feeling that they were "holding something back." "The Insidious Dr. Fu-Manchu" and all the rest had done their insidious work. At best (I used to think) they were a cold and reserved people; a people almost lacking in some of the characteristics which we have come to look upon as "human."

But when I went to China. . . .

THE HOUSEBOAT

CHAPTER I

1

SOMETHING had happened to the Pacific Ocean. The early sun, slowly freeing itself from the mists beyond the boiling, sinuous wake of the steamship, *Nanking,* disclosed a sea, not deep-sapphire as usual, but of a distinctly golden hue.

"Very muddy, isn't it?" said young Mr. Wong See Lo, who was standing beside me on the foredeck of the *Nanking*. Nevertheless, he turned his face eagerly toward the oncoming horizon; for here, after twenty days of sea and sky, was the Yangtze Kiang, that mightiest artery from the heart of China, sending its rich, alluvial flood fifty miles out to sea to greet us. For three hours the *Nanking* proceeded on her way, leaving behind her a trail of deepening color where the silt had risen to the churning of the propeller. Then, on the northern and southern horizons, appeared two faint blue lines lying parallel with the ship's course, and up over the sea's edge ahead of us came that stately, fantastic pageant of Oriental water craft which will always bring a thrill of wonder to the newcomer from the West. Great seagoing junks—galleons of the East—lay anchored at broad intervals along the shallow expanse of water or made way to the east or west under brown, heavy-hanging sails. Countless smaller junks, heeling over on their fat sides before the off-shore breeze, sailed with flat-keeled impunity over hidden shallows; while lorchas (those composite, not-altogether-happy sea sprites with European hulls and Asiatic batten lug sails) followed the channel guides with conscientious care. Tiny passenger sampans, bright as gaily colored lizards, skittered with quick tail-like wrigglings between the larger sea monsters. Ships of the West there were too, contrasting strangely in that amazing press of boats with round, staring eyes at their bows and writhing dragons painted on their carved, overhanging sterns.

Half an hour later the blue streaks of shore line converged into a wide river channel edged with wharves and factories, and the *Nanking,* steaming in past gunboats, tramps, junks, and battle cruisers, made fast to the floating docks of the international city of Shanghai.

Many things besides *ars et mores* have

changed since the year 300 B. C., when some long-forgotten emperor issued an edict giving the name, *Shanghai,* which means, *On the Sea,* to a sleepy settlement of fishermen's huts at the mouth of the Yangtze. That emperor would be considerably surprised if he could see the present location of his settlement. For the modern city of Shanghai lies thirteen miles up the Wangpoo River, the last affluent of the Yangtze; and it will continue to travel slowly inland as the Yangtze adds mile after mile to the broad edges of its mighty delta.

2

When Wong See Lo, with whom I shared a cabin on the *Nanking,* offered to initiate me into the mysteries of a Chinese hotel, his proposal was accepted with a pleasure very much like "the stern joy which warriors feel," for it was my sincerest wish not only to see the country which lay back of Shanghai, but to see it *Chinese-fashion.* The fact that I did not know just what Chinese-fashion meant— no stranger does until he tries it—only added the zest of experiment to an already well-developed enthusiasm. I had made solemn compact with myself not to attempt to describe, paint or otherwise molest the Imperial Palaces at Peking, but to see as much as I could of the Chinese people themselves in their humblest and most intimate surroundings. I had decided to use no letters of introduction, to live alone with the Chinese, and to eat their food.

Whether this *modus operandi* would work, I did not know. But there was one very good way to find out. . .

At the dock Wong See Lo and I climbed into a peculiar something mounted on four wheels, a pony squealed, and we clattered off over the cobblestones toward the Chinese hotel. The Bund, that splendid water-front avenue, with its trams, motor cars, tall buildings, and public gardens, was very much as one had expected—calm, dignified, expansive. But suddenly we turned into the city's main thoroughfare, Nanking Road; and just as suddenly the East rose up in its strength and submerged all memories of the West in a whirling, spinning vortex of pigtails, swinging gold signs, wheelbarrow men, dashing ricksha coolies, and high guttural cries. Instinctively I looked about for something solid, immobile, on which to rest the eyes. In all that seething torrent, the only stationary points were the vermilion turbans of the great Sikh policemen, who, in spite of their sad eyes, seemed to be smiling a serene, far-away smile into their black, evenly twisted beards.

The vehicle pulled up with a final flourish before the vast Oriental Hotel in the heart of the city. Very few foreigners put up at the Oriental—for reasons which I was to ascertain later. Reaching my room, I stepped out on to the narrow balcony, for the spell of the streets was still strong upon me. A billowing sea of gray, sharp-peaked roofs rolled off to the east, ending in a forest of masts and tall spars on the Wangpoo, a mile distant. In a window under the eaves of a house just across the way, a small point of light was shining from a dim lamp placed on a low stand well back in the room. Beside it, half-hidden by the curtains of a Chinese bed, reclined a gaunt, half-clad man deftly whirling a "pill" of opium over the steady flame! The East was more generous than had been reported in disclosing its secrets to the newcomer! I looked at my watch. The *Nanking* had been in dock just forty minutes.

3

That night Wong See Lo left by river

steamer for his home up the Yangtze, and the Oriental Hotel claimed me for its own. By day, with the aid of a phrase book in the Shanghai dialect and the hotel's compradore, or manager, I was largely occupied in trying to find a Chinese "cook boy" in whom "thought could wed itself to speech." By night the hotel itself furnished material for deep and solemn thought.

The partitions between the rooms consisted of thin, green wooden panels, which on the hall side ran up only to the top of the door. An airy, wooden trellis continued to the ceiling, allowing brilliant lights from the hall to shine through with a strength quite intense enough to permit a devout son of Han to read, if he chose, the ten treasonable offenses of the book of laws carved on a dime. This lighting arrangement was a very novel feature for those guests who wished to sit up in bed all night and read. It was also, I mused, a novel feature for those guests who did *not* wish to sit up all night and read. The bed itself was similar in form to an old-fashioned four-poster—curtains and all—but instead of having a spring, the bottom was made of split bamboo, interwoven like a cane-seated chair. Upon this firm foundation was a padded quilt with a sheet sewed to its *upper* side. Above was another quilt with a sheet sewed to its *under* side; so there could be no shadow of a doubt even in the mind of the most rural guest as to just where he fitted in.

On retiring to my room at eleven I remember thinking that the 26th of May must mark the celebration of a great national fête, but strangely enough, the guidebooks made no mention of it! There was no reason to doubt, however, that a jubilee of extensive proportions was taking place. For three hours I lay on my well-lighted bed listening fascinated to the strange cries, songs, and laughter from Nanking Road, and to the remarkable rhythm of a Chinese orchestra, squalling like a young Caliban on the hotel roof above my head. At two in the morning, other guests in adjoining rooms came trooping up to bed, and for the next hour, talked to each other across my green defenses in no uncertain tones, on topics about which they seemed to have pronounced, though diverse opinions. At last the voices died away. Well—it had been a good holiday, I hoped; and, moving a little to change the pattern of the interwoven bamboo on my shoulder blades,

I closed my eyes to see what could be done by counting sheep jumping over a fence. But lying there like Brunnhilde in a blaze of glory, I might just as well have tried to count ichneumons or even dinosaurs! From three o'clock on, perfect silence prevailed—except for the terrific, bronchial bark of a one-cylinder gasoline engine which reverberated up from the court below. At five o'clock its paroxysms, which had gradually become more and more violent, ended in a final, resounding snort, thus permitting a few fleeting moments of sleep before the song of the coolies welcomed in the rosy-fingered morn an hour later.

On the second night I was astonished to find that the festivities continued with all the abandon of the night before.

The third night, as I listened thunderstruck to the newly awakened noises from Nanking Road and the first peeps and toots which I had come to recognize as the tuning up of the orchestra, a light flashed over my somewhat jaded consciousness. This was no national fête! It was only the daily, humdrum existence of a Chinese hotel! And with that thought, I turned over, pulled the cotton quilt up about my ears, and fell into a solid, dreamless slumber. The first victory was won. As far as sleep was concerned I had become Chinese.

4

Then, quite unexpectedly, appeared—Ah Chow. He was a little old fellow with a long, pear-shaped head, the length of which was accentuated still more when he removed his hat by the appearance of a sudden black pompadour. A blue cotton gown enveloped his figure, and over his right eye was a large black patch which, on the whole, gave him a look decidedly less wicked than pathetic. One hand clutched a paper parasol and the other bore a note containing a few words of recommendation from a Chinese friend of Wong See Lo. Ah Chow, the note said, was no ordinary "boy," but could speak a language something like English, and was sure to give satisfaction.

I had already talked with a number of cook boys who were reported by the hotel's compradore to speak English, and to speak it "velly plopper"; but on trying to bring them down from beaming generalities about the weather to concrete arrangements about life, I had come up against such a wall of misunderstanding that Ah Chow, with comprehension flashing from his good eye and fairly familiar syllables on his lips, was *magnifique et pas cher;* so the matter was settled at once.

In central China there is just one best way of getting acquainted with one's Chinese neighbors. Take a houseboat! Accordingly, Ah Chow and I made our way to Soochow Creek, which after dividing Shanghai into halves, flows almost at right angles into the Wangpoo River. By going afoot we had the very great advantage of seeing the houseboat before its *lowdah,* or chief boatman, saw us, and in that way we would be able to approach in an unconcerned, offhand manner, which, Ah Chow said, was the necessary attitude for doing houseboat business with any sort of monetary satisfaction. After several fruitless trials, we came upon a boat of alluring appearance lying beside one of the bridges. The *lowdah* of the craft, a small, wiry man of grave appearance, with a moustache and goatee astonishingly like Napoleon the Third, was standing in the bow apparently wrapped in profound thought. (He told Ah Chow later that he had seen us coming half a mile away!) We therefore had no difficulty whatever in rousing him from his brown study—with the result that the boat

THE HOUSEBOAT

(together with the services of four boatmen who were to furnish their own meals) was engaged for one month. And the price—including a tip, or cumshaw, for all—was forty dollars! So, on the sixth morning—with two frying pans, one seaman's chest, one bedding roll, forty-four bundles of firewood and certain bags of provisions purchased by Ah Chow—we pulled in the gangplank, hove up the anchor and on the crest of the incoming tide, floated away up Soochow Creek for parts unknown.

The houseboat was a comfortable, shovel-nosed craft some thirty feet in length, with a small open deck at each end. The center was occupied by a low, ark-like superstructure which had a cabin at the forward part finished in some reddish, highly polished wood. It was scrupulously clean, and at the five narrow windows on each side hung crimson curtains which romped good-naturedly with the other red of the carved woodwork. There was an excellent bunk for the bedding-roll, and another which would hold the seaman's chest. There were two chairs, a table, a lamp, and a bookshelf (?) overhead. Back of the cabin was a room for Ah Chow, while the stern was occupied by the kitchen, and the boatmen.

From the water on both sides of the houseboat rose the mingling sounds of a vigorous river traffic. Junks, barges, and cargo-bearing houseboats lay moored in endless progression against the jetties, or, stirred to action by the rhythm of the great, finlike oar at side or stern, moved along the crowded waterway toward their destinations bearing ponderous loads of hemp, bean-cakes, wicker baskets, and matting. Others carried mixed cargoes of pigs, poultry, and garden vegetables, while still others were loaded down with great brown, earthen jars quite large enough to have housed any two of Ali Baba's stoutest gentlemen.

Napoleon (no other name suited the houseboat's *lowdah* so well) and his two sons, one large and one small, stood in the bow armed with long bamboo poles to prevent any possible intrusion of bridge-wall or passing river craft. Feeling a slight though regular undulation of the boat—as though it were being propelled by an oar in the stern—I looked around the end of the cabin toward the rear deck to see who the fourth boatman might be. At the long oar in the back stood two women! Trousered, it is true, but indisputably women! "Boatmen" was evidently a generic term in

This waterside building is a cloth merchant's warehouse! There is enough sketching material on the Grand Canal within two miles of Hang-Chow to keep a painter busy for years.

Napoleon's vocabulary! Later in the day I ventured a mild protest to Ah Chow on this peculiar *Ersheinung;* not that I objected particularly, but—

"Old man have got wife, have got daughter," explained Ah Chow. "Everybody live houseboat. What can do?"

"But the old man said, 'Four boatmen,' didn't he?" With wrinkled brow, Ah Chow began to count on uplifted fingers. "Old man, he one boatman; big son, he one boatman; litty son, he one boatman." He hesitated, and his eye roved, troubled, to mine.

"Yes," I encouraged, hiding some amusement which "litty son" had produced, "that makes three boatmen.

"Old man say," continued Ah Chow, resolutely, *"two lady, she make one boatman!"*

After that there was only one name for the houseboat with its "four boatmen" and its astonishing revelations. I call it the *Apocalypse.*

A few miles beyond Shanghai a slight breeze sprang up from the east and Napoleon piped the crew on deck in order to hoist a movable mast. Against this, a square sail braced with horizontal strips of bamboo was raised, and shortly we were moving along quite as fast as the carry-coolies and farm laborers who trotted down the towpath at our side. Soon the traffic lessened and the factories and tea houses facing the canal gave way to far-reaching rice fields dotted with groups of thatch-roofed houses under sheltering trees.

With the coming of night Napoleon found a mooring place at the intersection of two canals among a hundred other boats, which clustered together, not so much because they loved each other, but because they feared robbers more No sooner had we made fast than the *lowdah,* probably with the wisdom of experience, carefully tied up all the window latches with bits of string, and battened down the doors in a way that made mosquito netting quite superfluous; for no mosquito could have lived in the atmosphere which shortly resulted. After a very bad quarter-hour of partial anæsthesia, I decided that it was better to die gallantly in the open, fighting any number of robbers, than to strangle to death in that hermetically sealed wooden water-horse of Cathay. Then, too, for all I knew, the attack was quite as likely to come from the inside as the out. So after opening the windows to the great Chinese out-of-doors, I lay down to sleep with the consoling thought that it did not matter much where the trouble came from—for my nearest white neighbors were already twenty miles away.

5

When I awoke at dawn we were again under way. Napoleon and Dah Foo, the elder son, had taken a towline ashore, and were plodding steadily along on the towpath fifty feet ahead. The creek had broadened out into a tranquil, winding canal, along the irregular, grass-covered borders of which rose innumerable burial mounds and the broken columns of ancient *pai-lu*—those gray, dignified arches which China has so often raised in veneration of good women. Beyond lay rice field after rice field, yellow-topped and ready for the harvest—in June! Over the landscape rested that drowsy stillness which foretells the gentle and mature approach of summer. The canal lay mirror-like under the warm gray sky, while cargo boats and junks, visible on distant, parallel waterways, seemed to be moving like strange, detached phantoms across the open rice paddies. Blindfolded water buffalo, tended by little maids too small for any other work, plodded round and round like so many bovine Samsons at their wooden water wheels, or lolled neck-deep in the tepid water, occasionally exhaling huge breaths of lazy contentment.

Walking along the bank beyond the boatmen, I heard far ahead the sound of stalwart, childish voices, and a few minutes later along came five tiny, naked lads with yokes across their square little chests, pulling lustily on the towline of a small junk. On seeing me, they stopped their song abruptly, and when I stepped down from the towpath to make room for them, they hurried by in a decidedly nervous manner, only to break out (after they were well past) into a high chant that rang with the thrill of conscious victory.

Beyond a tapestry of glistening canals and decoratively grouped trees rose the mediæval battlements of the town of Quinsan. The sun, breaking through the clouds, sent broad shafts of light down a long vista of high-peaked bridges, sweeping gray-tiled roofs, canals, tea shops, and joss houses—a quaint stage-setting in which no two things-of-a-kind were alike except, perhaps, the ducks and the brown babies with shoe-button eyes and the huge earthen jars in front of the crockery shops. A crowd of little boys, shining like small, fiery gods in the late afternoon sun, scampered along the shore beside the houseboat with glad cries of discovery. What were they saying? I asked.

"One young fella say you have got blue eyes," said Ah Chow. "He say Chinese devils have got blue eyes. He say you *must* be devil!" Citizens of all ages foregathered on the bank—looking. One's face, so long unimportant, had suddenly become as compelling in interest as the face of an anteater or polar bear. Any slight movement of the facial muscles was hailed, if not with cheers, at least with, "Oh, did you see *that?*" or "Look at him *now!*" The immobile, expressionless countenance of my Chinese laundryman at home suddenly flashed before me, and I realized with a fine glow of understanding what had been the matter with his apparently ossified visage all these years. Most probably he looked that way because he had never wished to degenerate into a one-man menagerie for the youth of Washington Street!

Later, when the crowd had dispersed, I saw a small shaven head embellished with large, outstanding ears and set with a pair of jet-black eyes staring at me from the back of the houseboat. We were moored too far out in the canal for it to have been one of the little fellows from the shore. Who was it then? An additional "one-fourth boatman" thrown in by Napoleon for good measure?

Some time, I thought, when the opalescent dusk was not wrapping tower and turret of my first Chinese town in luminous wonder, and when a great star was not rising beyond the cypress-edged gateway of a Buddhist temple, I would take the time to find out just who my four boatmen might be. But now

> *. . . better to go silently*
> *To yon bridge-high trysting-place*
> *Where, in silence for a space*
> *You may look with upturned face*
> *On the face of Beauty, reading*
> *From her lips, and learning, heeding*
> *That, beyond the compassings*
> *Of teakwood toys, and glistening things*
> *Shine those rarer, fairer themes—*
> *Of Love, and Life, and Dreams.*

CHAPTER II

1

SWIMMING turtlelike, along the green surface of the canal, the *Apocalypse* turned noiselessly to the left and came to rest under the walls of the venerable city of Soochow. A group of ragged, mud-built huts—architectural counterparts of the beggars who occupied them—clustered about the city's western water gate. Stepping off of the gangplank, I passed between their dilapidated walls, went through a cavernous doorway, took two turns to the right, and found myself—in the *Arabian Nights!* Where but in that fantastic book could there be such a collection of brocades, ivories, translucent amber, glowing enamels, mud, cats, dogs, pigs, pearls, and smells? If Aladdin himself was not visible at the moment, it was only because he had just stepped into the neighboring goldsmith's shop to sell one of his silver plates! What pleasure, I thought, in all the world could compare with the joy of a certain young American I knew, just to be "let loose," absolutely loose, for one day in a

Chinese city? He would probably return to his parental roof with incipient cholera, malaria, and fleas; but, in his own vernacular, it would have been *"some* day"!

In the front of a small shop a calm-eyed wood carver, armed with mallet and chisel, was making the chips fly from a great wooden head of Buddha, as primitive and simple as the Sakyamuni himself. Beside him a helper glued together two huge blocks of wood to make the god's massive shoulders, while from a lower stratum among the shavings and bench legs an unthinkable din arose from the lusty throats of three puppies and four infants who were all quarreling together in the same common tongue. Next door, two goldbeaters, sitting vis-à-vis, pounded alternately with careful hammers upon the evenly laid "mold" of skins before them. No wonder they worked carefully. That small, rectangular pile of parchment on which they pounded was selected from the most delicate membranes of a hundred water buffalo! In a narrow shop beyond the goldbeaters, another infant, hardly large enough to hold a knife (to say nothing of wielding it), was cutting strips of bamboo for umbrella ribs, while his father, not at all averse to a little advertising, grinned amiably at the crowd which had collected, while he busily oiled the tops of his beautifully tinted paper umbrellas. A silversmith, setting emerald eyes into a silver dragon, chatted pleasantly with a butcher just across the way, in front of whose open shop the faces of six dead pigs, clean for the first time in their lives, hung white and ghostly like tragic masks in a row. "Varnished ducks," which, in spite of the calumny of the ages, are not varnished at all, but covered with an edible coating made of red rice,

> "Swung securely at their tether,
> Dancing merrily together"

to the clash of a neighboring brass shop, where numerous little scrubby-headed apprentices were pounding out heavy, beautifully proportioned brass bowls—unconscious works of art—to be sold at sixty-five cents each!

The narrow central street, fortified against the sun by bamboo mats stretched between the adjoining houses, opened directly into the glare of the wide, stone-paved court of the city temple beyond it. What was that suddenly returning memory of another dark, ambling "street of trinkets," and of standing blinded for a moment in the brilliant sunlight of just such another square, with a temple at the left and similar out-of-door cafés on either side? Strange—that Soochow with its Venetian network of canals should not only have its Piazza di San Marco but its Florian's as well!

Within the court, a fête was preparing. Peep shows and jugglers lined the balustrades before the temple, and beggars held up their wooden bowls to passers-by or muttered Lazarian supplications from the gateways. Energetic young Buddhist priests, whose shaved heads bore the twelve holy marks of their initiation, bustled here and there giving advice to novices who were making sacrificial horses, men, and boats of gaily colored paper pasted over rattan frames. Gentlemen of leisure, each with a bird cage in his hand, strolled about comparing the voices of their small captives or cracking the convivial melon seed together in the shade of their picturesque tea houses.

The temple across the square demanded investigation. In the semigloom of the outer court stood the Four Guardian Gods, two on each side, a savage and awe-inspiring quartet whose business it was to protect the mightier and calmer deities within. On a pedestal in their midst sat Mi La, the fat, jolly porter-god, extending his rotund face in a smile of good fellowship. A merry soul, Mi La, and thoroughly Chinese—so Chinese as to appear quite out of place among the four grim defenders of Indian origin who stood in threatening attitudes about him. What wise old priest, noting the depressing influence of these savage mercenaries on his peace-loving flock, had first interposed the smiling features and comfortable figure of Mi La at the outer gate to greet them as they entered?

Beyond a second sunlit court stood the inner sanctuary. I went forward toward the shadowed entrance, but at that moment a crash of gongs and a droning of horns, strange as Scottish bagpipes trying to play the airs of ancient Egypt, rose compellingly from the street in front of the temple. Joining the crowd, I caught a glimpse of white, blue, and gold banners, and the flicker of intense light as a dozen white-clad figures, riding shoulder-high in sedan chairs, came into the sunlight that flashed between the mats overhead.

"Somebody get married?" I asked Ah Chow, who was standing beside me.

"No," he answered, "somebody get dead."

White, then, in China was a sign of mourning! I must have shown my surprise, for a kindly look of solicitude appeared on Ah Chow's face.

"Married—dead," he said, "all the same!" I looked for a twinkle of humor in his good eye, but the side with the patch was toward me.

"Are you married, Ah Chow?" I asked.

"Long, long time," he said, gravely. "Maybe you married too?"

2

The charm of its gardens alone would give Soochow high claim to distinction; and particularly among its gardens, the garden Lu Yuen. For the cool fragrance of Lu Yuen rests like an aura of beauty over the more strident memories of that typically Chinese city.

One entered the garden by passing through three small, white rooms, undecorated except for a row of circular windows, set with stone tracery, through which other simple, white walls were visible. This chaste prelude had doubtless been planned with painstaking care, for it was as graceful as the first gently thrummed notes of a moon guitar under the fingers of a singing-girl. In a white alcove upon the left, filled with sky and sunlight, a dwarfed tree, holding by slender roots to the crevices of an aged, gray rock, pointed the way to a row of shining black columns and a sun-flooded archway beyond. One felt that the fingers of the singing-girl had finished the prelude, and that her song was beginning. Sitting beside a thicket of bamboo in the garden, I jotted down such broken fragments of that song as came to me:

> *Doorways,*
> *Circular and octagonal. . . .*
>
> *Blue shadows of camphor trees*
> *Playing across a jade-green pool*
> *Where diaphanous-tailed goldfish*
> *Rest beneath broad leaves. . . .*
>
> *Blackbirds, singing against red*
> * blossoms. . . .*
>
> *Two peacocks*
> *By an ivory-white balustrade*
> *Moving silently among black*
> * columns. . . .*

But when I had written these lines, I closed my notebook. For it was not the song of the garden I was writing, but only words; and I realized a little sadly that the true loveliness of the melody itself could not be carried away, but must remain where it belonged, inseparable from the rhythm of the sunlit branches and the wind playing among the trees.

3

Sleeping profoundly one night at Soochow, we were awakened by the furious pounding of a small gong. Other gongs, high and shrill, added their rapid tap-tap-tap, chiming in like a chorus of startled machine guns, until the night seemed lost in a clamor of brazen sound. From the windows of the *Apocalypse,* we could see flames shooting up above the roofs on the opposite side of the canal not more than a hundred yards away. Sparks were lighting all around us, and a wild welter of junks and houseboats surged down the waterway. Napoleon, being uninsured, was inclined to seek safety in flight, but was finally persuaded that since retreat meant the certain breakage of rigging, valor was, in this case, the better part of discretion. So, sending the younger son up on top of the cabin roof to keep off any stray sparks, we held fast and watched the spectacle.

Firemen, clad like gladiators fresh for com-

THE HOUSEBOAT 41

bat in uniforms consisting of shoes, loin-cloths and glittering, high-crested helmets, sprang shouting to their work, muscles rippling and bronze skins shining in the red glare of the fire. Pump company after pump company dashed up, and the massed crowds on the flame-illumined street along the canal quickly separated into tossing groups, as each company, working like a thing demented at the double handle of its old-fashioned hand pump, tried to send its stream of water higher into the blaze than the others. Torchbearers, rushing along the water front, and half-clad axmen in their classic helmets, climbing over the roofs and brandishing their weapons against the flames, brought the uncanny feeling that one was witnessing the burning of Rome. To add to the eerie effect, some gentleman of Neroesque reactions in one of the houses upon our own side of the canal was playing a merry but bizarre tune upon a Chinese fiddle.

As the fire showed no signs of abating, I took a ferry boat across the canal to see whether there might not be something of interest nearer at hand. On a street corner, very much in the way, and directly in the heat of the blaze, stood a group of four citizens—drinking tea! A helmeted fireman dashed up, made a report, received some calmly delivered instructions, and dashed off again. Fire chiefs! Water from thirty hose nozzles was playing on the blaze, but much of the volume was lost because of the decrepit state of the hose, some sections of which were bandaged along their entire length with pieces of rag and string. Where the rags had given away, small boys stood with thumbs and fingers pressed tightly over the holes, exactly like Chinese versions of the story of the Dutch boy who saved the dike. Fortunately there was little wind, and as Chinese city roofs are usually of tile, the fire after satisfying its appetite on a small block of houses, burned itself into a heap of glowing embers. I returned to the boat.

"To-morrow," said Ah Chow by way of greeting, "plenty people never burn red candle like every day. More better somebody burn yellow candle to Fire Joss."

For beyond the shadow of a doubt, the much dreaded Fire Joss was responsible for it all!

4

By slow degree, an inventory, or more properly, a census of the human contents of the *Apocalypse* became possible. There was Napoleon, of course, and the big son whose name was Dah Foo, which happily means "mate." Then there was the smaller son with a name which sounded something like "Umpah," and that hybrid but efficient "fourth boatman" consisting of Mrs. Napoleon and Mrs. Dah Foo. There were also two tiny boys, sons of Dah Foo, and a large man with bulbous cheeks and a gold watch chain who squatted by the hour on the back deck smoking a long pipe— a second-cabin passenger, I judged, for he landed at one of the villages beyond Soochow and did not appear on board again. The only mystery connected with him was, where did he sleep? I got the dimensions of the back of the boat and sitting down for an idle half-hour, I tried to plot out the possible sleeping space for those eight people. Geometry and ethics both agreed that it could not be done. The stranger was a part of the picture-puzzle that refused to fit. I gave it up. Perhaps he draped himself over the long oar. Perhaps he slept on the charcoal stoves. . . .

Into that same limited space, food was taken from the cabin to be prepared by Ah Chow. On several occasions, it appeared (in a vague, intangible way) that considerably more provender was going from the larder into the unexplored region of the charcoal stoves than could possibly be consumed by a single white man, were he Dr. Johnson himself. In fact, I began to fancy that I was running a small floating hotel, American plan. However, as I have a rather suspicious and unpleasant nature, I resolved for once to rise above myself and keep my thoughts unsullied as long as I could. But one day as Ah Chow was taking potatoes—many potatoes—out of a large sack which was cached under the berth, I looked at the kettle he was filling, and my self-respect bade me speak.

"Ah Chow," I said, resolutely, "fifteen potatoes are altogether too many for my dinner."

He looked at me with gentle astonishment. "Chinee potato very queer," he said, wistfully. "Boil him a few moment, he shrink very litty."

Possibly so, possibly so! China, in some respects, *is* a strange country. . . .

5

Matters of great interest lay near Soochow. Foremost among them, at a place where six canals joined together in a wide expanse of water, was a great stone bridge called the Bridge of the Precious Girdle. Looking down its long vista of fifty-three arches set with stone lions, and seemingly fastened to the land at each end by two small iron pagodas, one imagined that the name was only a pleasing allusion to its successful girding of the waters. But legend relates that in the distant time of the Tang Dynasty, when funds for the completion of the bridge were lacking, the governor of Soochow gave his jeweled belt of office in order that the work might be carried to a triumphant close. And so, with that rare instinct which has transmuted so many Chinese names into epigrams, they called it the Bridge of the Precious Girdle.

According to Ah Chow, there was an ancient tradition which affirmed that whoever counted the arches of the bridge beginning at the south end would count fifty-two arches instead of fifty-three. And while I counted, he waited with a look of such expectant delight on his battered old face that I did not have the heart to tell him my count was the same from both ends; so he went off in high glee to spread the news of the potency of the tradition to Napoleon and the rest—especially to the "fourth boatman," who were always having their fortunes told, and who had a pronounced leaning toward the occult.

Often came the strange impression, as in certain scenes in *Parsifal,* that the houseboat was stationary and that the country itself was gliding by, disclosing its fairest treasures. Shi-men, Wu-si, Wu-kiang, Ka-shing—walled cities these of deep and ancient charm, each with its own inimitable temple or bridge or pagoda—flowed past in dazzling, colorful progression. Phases of life unimagined in the Occident greeted the eye at every turn, simple and yet astonishing. The very canal bottom furnished livelihood for thousands of dwellers in miniature houseboats who scraped it for water weeds, prodded it for mussels, and dug up its mud for fertilizer.

In the stern of a sampan no larger than a small rowboat sat a man of perhaps twenty, digging at the canal bottom with a wooden scoop fastened to the end of a bamboo pole. Bringing it to the surface, he emptied its contents into a sieve held by his young wife at the other end of the boat, who washed the mud out of it, and then, sorting it over by hand, picked out and saved the small pieces of unburnt coal

The business men of Ka-shing come to this island tea-house for a day in the open—playing dominoes.

which had been thrown overboard in the *ashes* of the passing steam launches! *That* was their living, and the sampan, with its cabin made of movable matting, was their home. In a few months there would be snow on the ground, and ice would be floating on the water, but if they were like Dah Foo and Napoleon and the others, they would continue to sift their coals without complaint. And when the Chinese New Year came they would rejoice with the rest of China, not for the year that was to come, but with grateful hearts that they had successfully gone through the months that had passed!

Would anyone, I wondered, who had seen these things be content to remain the remote and analytical traveler, interested only in matters of politics and state, and the study of long-forgotten dynasties? Perhaps—

But at that moment there came to my eyes the portent of a not-far-distant event which the young girl sitting tranquilly in the bow of the boat made no effort to conceal. And suddenly, tears were in my eyes. For this was a symbol of faith and hope that transcended the proudest story of the mightiest dynasty of kings.

CHAPTER III

1

WE were sailing down the Grand Canal with a spanking breeze bulging out the brown, bamboo-ribbed sail above us. Napoleon stood Gibraltar-like at the tiller, stern and grave under the responsibility of taking his craft through the water at the astonishing speed (for a houseboat) of five miles an hour. But his imperial frisked merrily in the breeze, and the other boatmen hugged themselves in quiet glee. Six hours of such traveling would save two days of arduous towing!

Straight as a boulevard before us lay the Grand Canal. Starting at Tien-tsin, nine hundred miles to the north, it had traversed the valley of the Yellow River, cut the Yangtze at Chin-kiang, and, mingling with a closely woven network of smaller canals, was now carrying the houseboat to the city of Hang-chow at its southern extremity. For thirteen centuries, boats identical in pattern with those about us had been sailing on this man-built waterway. A little to the north one section of the canal had gone into operation when Xerxes was gathering his Medes and Persians for that invasion of Greece which gave the world Thermopylæ. In the course of the ages, the canal seemed occasionally to have stirred in its bed, for very often one of the arches of a three-spanned bridge would not be functioning over the water at all, but over the land.

At a small waterside village, what was my surprise to hear two carry-coolies singing with great accuracy this short theme used by Puccini in *Madame Butterfly:*

The Italian maestro had evidently traced his themes to their original sources! The coolies, it is true, were in China while the opera was laid in Japan. But Japanese music, like every other Japanese art, is based on the Chinese. No doubt the same theme is to be heard to-day in the rice paddies north of Tokyo.

The *Apocalypse* being very unwieldy, great vigilance was necessary in steering among the innumerable junks and barges which clustered beside the semicircular stone bridges along the canal. In order to pass under the low arches, it was always the rule to drop the sail and lower back the mast, an operation which required a certain nicety of care and judgment. At such times Napoleon resigned the tiller to his wife, and took station at the bow with a long pole, to guard with his life, if necessary, the varnished sides of the houseboat. Dah Foo handled the sail, while Umpah, the smaller son, lowered back the mast over the cabin. At one of the bridges, Umpah unfortunately started to lay back the mast before his brother had quite dropped the sail. That evidently was not houseboat etiquette, for Napoleon fetched him a clip over the top of his black, velvety head with the handle end of the pole, which in another country would probably have called for ambulance service and the Juvenile Protective Association. But Umpah only wiggled his ears a bit, looked a little hurt that I should have witnessed the scene—and the incident was closed.

Umpah and I were fast becoming very well acquainted. At first he was a little shy, but our *camaraderie* took a firm footing when, on accidentally setting a plate down on a palette full of wet paint, he found that I did not explode then and there and sink the ship as he apparently expected. After that, we held daily conversations together (each in his native tongue) on such matters as the size and population of towns, the home ports of the junks we passed en route, and the position of cities and stars with reference to the points of the compass. He explained to me very clearly, without understanding a word of English, that when the stars twinkled in the evening there was likely to be a breeze the following day—a fact with a sound scientific basis of which I was not at the time aware. First came the word "twinkle" (expressed by quickly winking the eyes and pointing to the stars). Then came "the next day" (shown by closing the eyes, snoring a little, opening the eyes, and then by making a large circle with the tips of the fingers, slowly rising from the east). And, finally, the word "breeze" was made by puffing out the cheeks, after the boisterous manner of Eolus, Boreas, and the rest.

All of which is additional testimony to that unquiet thought which bothers each of us occasionally—that if all the Umpahs in the world could have other people's advantages, a good many of those other people with advantages might very shortly have to make way for the Umpahs.

2

Though the *Apocalypse* was never more than a few yards from land, we experienced adventures amusingly like those of mariners on

> "The sea! the sea! the open sea!
> The blue, the fresh, the ever free!"

When the wind was good we rejoiced. Often when we were becalmed there was nothing for it but to get out the oars. Once we stuck on a mud bank and suffered shipwreck with water rising in the cabin. Like some of Conrad's seafaring men, we forgot the day of the week, the name of the month, and what year it was. When Napoleon was consulted about the weather he would consider the points of the compass with such gravity that the heavens seldom had the temerity to do other than he suggested. When a heavy wind bellied out the square, bamboo-strung sail, his face assumed lines of mastery almost Seawolfesque, and he bellowed his orders to the crew—ladies and all —in a voice that brooked no lingering over dominoes or rice bowl. As the weather grew warmer he appeared one morning in his summer costume consisting of a blue shirt (tails out Chinese-fashion), a pair of white knee-pants and a round, tight skull cap with a button on the top like that of a college freshman. The goatee and the gravity remained, but the combination of that *phantasie* below and that face above was so uproarious, that for several days whenever he hove in sight, I had to busy myself with many things in order not to commit an indiscretion.

Umpah and Dah Foo stripped down to a pair of trousers each, only putting on a coat at dinner to keep off the mosquitoes. For there *were* mosquitoes. Before leaving Shanghai I had purchased a Japanese mosquito net, but, unfortunately, the holes were either constructed to keep out a more heavily built insect, or else the thrifty manufacturers were trying to save material, for morning would disclose a dozen or more stodgy, plethoric mosquitoes, who, like the wolf of the Brothers Grimm, had been able to get in, but after dining, could by no means get out. On my showing them to Ah Chow, he regarded their obeseness with great disdain and said, "Oh, him very fat! No can fly!" without appearing to realize that they had reached their debased, Falstaffian condition by dining on the person of his employer.

Napoleon, who had a vast knowledge of the countryside, would usually drop anchor where the mosquitoes were comparatively few, but occasionally they would mobilize in strength, and then—antiphonal to the clash of wings of the first hundred thousand—would arise a symphony of "mosquito smudges" quite beyond description. In the cabin, I used a sort of Japanese punk stick—rank enough, goodness knows—but efficient. Ah Chow burned a Chinese product which distinctly reeked of poison gas, while from the back of the *Apocalypse* came an effluvium warranted, like a Colt .45, not only to stop a man but to knock him down.

Thus, houseboating was not all paradise. When there was no better stopping place, we moored for the night in pools of green slime where, perhaps, goats, rikshas, and rice were all washing at the same time. Sometimes, in the presence of fragrances that arose from a Chinese village under the noonday sun, one would be forced to fly in utter defeat. The man who said, "See Naples and die—of its smells," is the merest rookie in nasal combat!

But, after all, what of it? Man is not made

with a scullion soul that is susceptible only to dirt! Where in the world—in the Western world—could one stand before a carpenter shop, breathing the pungent, aromatic scent of camphor and camellia and Japanese cedar? And where could one see the mist over the rice paddies and hear the calm song of the rain-bird telling the straw-cloaked coolies of the approaching shower?

3

A magnificent three-arched bridge announced our arrival in the outskirts of the city of Hang-chow. Napoleon, it seemed, had been born on a junk in the very shadow of that bridge, but he showed no particular emotion upon seeing it again except to announce his patronage by roaring, *"Baaza!"* which means "Pull on the long oar," or *"Taysa!"* which means "Push on it," in more stentorian tones than ever to the crew. A day or two earlier he had presented me with an ultimatum to the effect that he was not going to take the houseboat back to Shanghai at all, but intended to remain indefinitely at Hang-chow. That was the one vulnerable point in our agreement. In my complete ignorance I had imagined that houseboats always returned to their original starting-point; so now I looked forward to seeing myself, together with much impedimenta, standing in a boatless and chaotic condition upon the jetty at Hang-chow.

Two miles beyond the bridge, the Grand Canal ended abruptly in a great cluster of warehouses and shipping, while Hang-chow itself, unlike any other city we had passed, lay an additional two miles away from the canal, and was only connected with it by narrow waterways too small to accommodate the *Apocalypse*. So moorings were found near the bridge.

"It is higher than all cities in the world in point of grandeur and beauty as well as from its abundant delights, which may lead an inhabitant to imagine himself in Paradise." Such was Marco Polo's impression of Hang-chow in the year 1392. The other extreme came in 1861, when during a siege by the Taiping rebels, human flesh was publicly sold in the streets for food! While Hang-chow of to-day has lost all trace of the glory described by the famous Venetian, it shows a vast improvement over Taiping days. Passing along its smaller streets, one was constantly reminded by the rattle and thunder of its looms that it was *par excellence* the city of silk. Probably no other city in the world could boast of ten thousand stands of hand looms and eight thousand high-grade weavers; and I use the word "boast" intentionally. For there are certain matters, beginning at the top with the Nikē *Victory* and coming right down to homely, delightful things like muffins and mince pie, which—even if the world should last a million years—will never be made quite as well by machinery as by human hands.

4

The happy Chinese faculty for using graphic and ornamental names is nowhere more happily displayed than on the shores of Lake Si-wu, which lies directly to the west of Hang-chow. "Day-dawn Bell on Nan-ping Hill," "Spring Dawn at Su-ti," "Cloud-holding Twin Peaks," "Wavelike Willows to hear Golden Orioles"—these names and many more made a tranquil and pleasing preparation for the scenes they described. Green islands, ivy-crowned temples, moss-covered grottoes where willows drooped like motionless fountains over silent pools, brought the sudden intuitive sense that the story of the Chinese Nightingale could have taken place at no other spot than this.

"In China, as you know," the story begins, "the Emperor is Chinese, and all around him are Chinese also"; and then it goes on to tell how the Emperor read in a book describing his garden that the song of the nightingale was "best of all," and how he sent his chancellors to look for it; and how they searched in vain for a long time. "But at last," it continues, "they met a poor little girl in the kitchen who said, 'Oh! the nightingale! I know her very well. O how she can sing! Every evening I carry the fragments left at the table to my mother who is sick. And when I am coming back, and stay to rest a little in the wood, I hear the nightingale sing. It is just as though my mother had kissed me. . . .'

" 'Little kitchen maid,' said the chief chancellor, 'I will procure for you a high appointment, together with permission to see his Majesty the Emperor dine, if you will conduct us to the nightingale. . . .'" So the story continues, transmuted by Hans Andersen into the purest gold. And if the years have not done bitter and sad things to us, we may read and enjoy it still.

THE HOUSEBOAT

Like a far sentinel against the blue hills, an ancient, half-ruined pagoda rose from a thicket of live oak at the southern end of the lake. The Queen of Wu, who built it, did not know that more than a thousand years later, country women would come from far and near to pick up fragments of its bricks as talismans to make their silk worms bear more excellent silk. In a valley by the pagoda a Buddhist monastery called to me with glistening orange walls. Gray-garmented monks were busily engaged about its inclosures making mud idols, and setting them up in the sun to dry. On entering the temple with its frowning guardsmen and its ever-laughing Mi La (he is said to have died of laughter), a heavy, unfamiliar fragrance, very different from the usual scent of incense, came to the nostrils. In the stately central chamber its presence was quickly explained. Sitting in a row upon their newly carved pedestals were three colossal gods of Indian sandalwood. They were as yet unlacquered, and the huge, carefully matched joints at their shoulders and along the sides of their heads were quite visible. To an Occidental who had always associated sandalwood with fans, jewelry boxes, and other *res feminæ,* the sight of three massive, thirty-foot gods carved out of twelve-inch sandalwood timbers was something of a shock! Passing through a second courtyard, under the guidance of a short, jovial-looking friar, we turned to the right, and after winding in and out among a number of monastic buildings, arrived before a small chapel which was presided over by a smiling, gilded Joss, unlike any other I had seen, with outstretched hand pointing downward to the mouth of a well in the floor directly in front of him. The fat little priest stopped, folded his hands over his *moyen-age* stomach, and told the following tale, which was immediately translated by Ah Chow with great enthusiasm and gusto:

5

Several hundred years ago, some itinerant Buddhist friars traveling from the south, decided to make their home in the small village in this green valley beside the lake. Though they had nothing of their own, and wished for nothing, they quickly inspired in the hearts of the villagers a desire for a large and handsome temple. There were many willing hands to work with great fervor in the erection of the edifice, but materials were woefully lacking—especially the mighty beams and pillars which to this day form the framework of all Chinese temples. The nearest supply of such wood was hundreds of *li* away in the forests of Fuhkien—which might just as well have been *ultima Thule* as far as the slender pocketbooks of the villagers were concerned.

Just at that time there appeared in their midst a strange friar so unprepossessing in appearance and manner as to serve, in a small way, to take the thoughts of the villagers from their greater sorrow. In the first place, strangers were not particularly popular in those days unless they came very highly recommended. And in the second place, this particular stranger had traits which could not be passed over lightly, even in a friend. Professing to be a friar, he by no means restricted himself to a diet of bean curd and cabbage as he should have done, but whenever he was invited out—and that wasn't often—he ate heavily of beef and pork, and had even been seen to drink copiously of the fermented juice of the rice. He was lazy and shiftless, and had never even been known to take a bowl of water and go through the motions of bathing as other people did; and, worst of all, he was always smiling.

"See here, scaramouch," said the villagers at last, "if you can't help us out of our difficulty, you should at least have the decency to refrain from grinning like an ape all over the place! It is far from considerate, and besides, it distracts us from our sorrow."

"What's the trouble?" asked the monk.

Tzing-pe! Just as though the fellow didn't know what the matter was! It would serve him right if the Head Friar made him bring the timbers from Fuhkien to the village one by one on his back!

For once the monk became serious. "O-ho!" he said, "if it's timbers you want, I'm your man." And with that, he disappeared.

The next event in the story occurred early in the morning near the great forests of Fuhkien on the estate of a rich though very selfish lady named Wu. The lady Wu had not slept very well, because all night long there had been a terrible noise of nasal singing in the courtyard outside of her window, accompanied by the monotonous banging of a *lo* and the vile squeaking, not of the wry-necked fife, but of the badly tuned *tinken,* which, if anything, is a little worse. Instead of stopping at dawn as most noises in China do, it continued well into the morning with increased vehemence, so that at last she sent her *amah* out to ascertain the cause of the uproar.

"There is a wandering friar in the courtyard who requests a favor of you," said the *amah*.

Now, among the lady's better qualities was an inclination toward charity which her parsimonious nature, however, had never allowed to get any further than a suppressed reflex. It would not cost anything, she thought, to find out what the friar wanted. So she invited him in and gave him what welcome a great lady might, asking him in due time what he desired.

"Only as much wood as I can wrap in my cloak," said the friar.

The idea of giving anything away was not to the lady's liking; but after considerable demurring, she consented and the friar made for the woods where he wrapped his cloak about one great tree after another with lightning rapidity. No sooner had he encircled a tree than it disappeared into the ground with a noise like thunder!

The lady Wu arrived breathless on the scene just as he was covering the trunk of the last tree, and immediately began to upbraid him. But at that moment the friar expanded to gigantic proportions and said, "This is only a just repayment for your selfishness." Thereupon, the lady at once fell on her knees and "wept piercingly, shedding the warm tear."

"But," added the friar, softening a little, "since you were not entirely ungenerous, the forest will regain its former height in three years' time. Meanwhile, you will do well to ponder over your selfish ways." Again he vanished, only to reappear a day or two later in the village beside the lake, smoking his long pipe and smiling just as foolishly as before.

"Well, braggart, have you the wood?" asked the villagers, by way of greeting.

"*Well*—yes," he replied, cracking a melon seed.

"Where is it then?" they demanded.

"In the *well*," he answered, cackling at his bad joke.

More as a reason for making him out a simpleton than because they believed him, they lowered a candle into the well, and sure enough, there was the end of a great, squared timber sticking a foot out of the water. No sooner had they rigged up a derrick and hoisted it out, fifty men straining on the bamboo cable, than another timber appeared in its place. Before long, an enormous pile of wood lay beside the proposed site of the temple.

"Have you enough timber?" asked the friar, smiling at the chief carpenter.

"Yes, your Worship," said the chief carpenter, bobbing up and down; for by this time, all the village knew that the friar was a Joss. But the chief carpenter, being somewhat a-twitter at talking to a Joss, had made a slight error in his figures, so that when it came to putting on the roof, one great girder was lacking.

"There is still a timber in the well," said the friar, grinning at the villagers (who naturally enough grinned right back at him).

Then they set up the derrick again, and the fifty men strained at the bamboo cable, but without avail. So they put sixty men, seventy men on the cable, and finally the whole village lent a hand, but they only broke the rope without budging the timber.

"Never mind," said the friar at last. And that night in the temple by himself, he rolled up a lot of shavings, and kneaded them together, and then pulled them out into a huge timber, after which he disappeared forever, leaving the other log still stuck in the well.

. . . . . .

The little Buddhist priest unfolded his hands, took up a candle which lay beside him, lighted it, and carefully lowered it by a long cord into the opening before us. We leaned over and watched it intently as it went down—thirty, forty, fifty feet. The candle stopped. There, protruding a foot above the black surface of the water, was the end of a great squared timber rising up solidly from the bottom of the well!

And when you go to the temple called Tzu Tain Sen, by the old pagoda at the south end of Lake Si-wu, be good enough, if you will, to bear out this story by looking down the well and seeing the timber for yourself.

6

For two weeks I painted from the deck of the houseboat near the end of the Grand Canal, where an old Ming temple, surrounded by mighty trees, rose high above the jetty at the water's edge. Here too was the nightly mooring place of the houseboat, for here the noise from the tea houses and samshu shops which

The undefinable beauty of a Chinese night can only be suggested. One must conjure up the mysterious, brooding spirit of the East. . . .

skirt Hang-chow lost themselves down a mile of sleeping junks, and the broad mirror of the canal lay still and silent, reflecting the stars. On calm nights—and most Che-kiang nights in June are calm—the white walls of the temple fashioned other white walls in the quiet water, and the massive patterns of dark-tiled roofs cut great simple designs across the sky. Sometimes, during the silent hours before morning, came the sound of a voice, a solitary singing voice, which wove like a shining thread into the fiber of one's dreams. Whose voice it was I did not know. It seemed to have great beauty—but, of course, when one is half asleep sounds often take on a quality which they do not actually possess. The only way to judge of its illusive charm was to hear it with all the senses awake.

So, sitting out on deck one night, I waited. Dah Foo and the younger brother slept peacefully in their summer quarters on the roof of the cabin a few feet away. As usual, the night was calm and clear. Small fishes, hungry perhaps for the stars which swam like silver crescents upon the black surface of the canal, jumped with crisp splashes in the silence. In a far-off lane a dog barked once, twice, thrice, but the fast-beating pulses into the cabin to find a Chinese flute (which Dah Foo had taught me to play), so that I might more easily remember the notes I had just heard. But while I was groping around in the darkness, the singer changed back to the first theme, and the other, being more ephemeral, was gone.

I listened until the voice died away; and I listened on other nights before leaving the houseboat; but that fugitive music of enchantment was not repeated. After all, I thought, it was perhaps composed of those curious intervals which in certain Oriental music lie somewhere between the tones of our own less flexible scale. Or perhaps—and who knows?—it was one of those beautiful, solemn affirmations which sometimes come to each of us, and which we meet with yearning hearts, seeking to pierce the mystery of that other world that lies all around us—a world transcended by a beauty more exquisite than that which we already know.

RIVER CITIES

CHAPTER IV

1

THE separation from the houseboat was accomplished with no trouble at all. The *Apocalypse* merely pulled alongside the trailer of a steam launch, boxes and canvases were transferred to the trailer by careful hands (how different from the land of the free and the home of the brave!), kindly farewells were said, and three days later we stood once more in the lobby of the Oriental Hotel.

On the houseboat there had been too much baggage. One's head had been in the clouds, but one's feet had been chained to an incubus beginning with a granite water pitcher and ending with the matronly figure of a large bedding-roll.

"This time," I said aloud, "we will cut down the baggage to the nth power!"

"How say?" asked Ah Chow, politely, at my elbow.

"This time, make one trip up Yangtze River on Chinese steamer. Travel Chinese-fashion. This time, take very few box. Can do?"

"Can do," said Ah Chow, promptly.

At three o'clock the next afternoon a small parade of rickshas was standing in front of the Oriental Hotel. Two which were to carry Ah Chow and myself were empty, but the other three were loaded down with *seven* great pieces of baggage. "We are seven," they seemed to say with smug complacency.

"Why have got so big baggage?" I demanded of Ah Chow, to whom the details of packing had been left.

"I thought-so you say, 'Take very few *box.*' This time, *no have got box!*"

True, alas! No "box," but seven large bags! No time to change now! The steamer would be leaving in half an hour. With hoarse shouts the ricksha men dashed off down Nanking Road in a formation not unlike the ancient Greek phalanx. Pedestrians skittered away from us with the nicely timed judgment of poultry on the Lincoln Highway. A Hindu policeman, probably reacting to prenatal memories of the Car of Jagannath, stopped all traffic for half a block to let us pass. Other rickshas hesitated, and then darted timidly away from the approaching apex of the flying wedge. Turning to the right into a quieter street, the ricksha men, now running as silently as a flock of large ostriches, traversed the narrow French Concession, and reaching the wide Avenue des Deux Républiques, continued down toward the water front where a large Chinese river steamer was lying. Just as we came aboard, the whistle bellowed its final warning, the shouting coolies cast off the hawsers, and the steamer, plowing downstream amid the noises of an immense water traffic, added one more swiftly moving fragment to the surging kaleidoscope of the harbor.

Ahead of us, six majestic, fantastically painted ocean-junks, like rotund foreign ambassadors at the court of Elizabeth, lay moored about a trim, elegant yacht. Just to the left five hundred half-clad coolies sweated and sang among a mountain of bales on the jetties, while not a hundred feet from the coolies, in a public garden, groups of fair-haired, pink-cheeked children, as lovely as those in Central Park or the Luxembourg, played among brilliant beds of asters in the shade of high, well-kept trees! (Any painter, I thought, who attempted that sweep of water front would be accused of Futurism of the deepest dye!)

Thirteen miles below Shanghai, we passed

the famous Wusung fortifications—the Fort Sumter of the Chinese Republic—and then, turning on a wide arc to the left, we saw about us a vast, familiar expanse of golden water. We had left the Wangpoo and were sailing on the broad bosom of the Mighty One, the Son of the Sea, the Yangtze Kiang.

It is clear that the great Jinn of the river must have a very kindly regard for the pigmy, Man, who for a hundred centuries has spread his matting sails on its tawny breast in numbers that have made the Yangtze the most valuable waterway in the world. But in spite of past æons of junk traffic, its day is only beginning. The time is not far off when the great river—already an international highway—will carry a trade in comparison with which the whole history of China's foreign commerce will sink into insignificance. "The romance of trade," to quote every sea writer since Raleigh, "is a never-ending romance." True, the galleons no longer come bowling in loaded to the "gunnels" with doubloons, and Captain William Kidd and the Brothers Lafitte no longer send a thrill of wild adventure down the spines of voyageurs. But a careful perusal of Lloyd's Foreign Register and the International Shipping News will show that the best men and the best ships still win. No matter where or how we are chained, *that* is still of interest to all of us—for whether the distant cry comes to us out of Homer's *Odyssey,* or Conrad's *Youth,* or Masefield's *Dauber,* or in the great thundering voice of the ocean itself, the call of far countries will always be the same, and will always bring the same far-yearning, unfulfilled desire to the hearts of men.

2

The cost of "foreign-style" traveling to Hankow, six hundred miles up the Yangtze, is forty dollars. To travel the same distance "Chinese fashion" costs seven dollars and a half. My "Chinese-fashion" cabin was small but clean. There were three bunks, two of which were unoccupied during the entire journey. Meals were served upon a portable table, and a steward who had only one other cabin was in almost constant attendance. Hot water arrived automatically in the morning, tea was replenished at short intervals during the day, and every need was met with the most willing and courteous service that could be expected from one mortal to another. The meals on board were, of course, Chinese—great quantities of rice, bean sprouts, some sort of shellfish, pork with dried bamboo shoots, cabbage, and tea. Ah Chow, who at his own suggestion had taken a third class ticket for two dollars and ten cents (imagine traveling six hundred miles for two dollars and ten cents!), found that he knew a "ship fella" on board, and so slept very comfortably at night in the saloon of the first cabin.

Sixty-five miles above the river's mouth, a long island which seemed to be the left bank, came to an end and the Yangtze broadened out into an immense expanse of water that merged on the north, east and west into the horizon. But soon the left bank itself appeared in the far distance bounded by vast plains which in turn were girded by rugged mountain ranges. Small mud-colored villages wallowed in the ooze (inundated this year, as every year), while their inhabitants sat philosophically on the bank higher up waiting for the waters to fall. Huge, isolated crags, temple-crowned giants of the Paleozoic time, thrust themselves two hundred, three hundred feet out of the rushing water.

At every port the steamer's gangways

swayed under a seething mass of incoming and outgoing bales, boxes, matting-wrapped bundles, and human beings. Hawkers crying their nondescript wares swarmed over the gunwales and up the cables on the ship's side. Rye-paste cakes, red pills, cold arrowroot jelly, rag dolls, and long, twisted crullers quickly reduced the available coppers of the many "space passengers," whose grass sleeping-mats lined the deck in front of the cabins.

One elderly peddler, finding that I did not look with favor on his sodden refreshments, put down his basket, and fishing in an inner pocket, unearthed a battered package of chewing gum which he presented to me with a look of sympathy and understanding that brooked no refusal. Another—this time a youngster—gave me a Chinese paper to read, but seeing that I did quite as well with it upside down as the other way, he righted it for me, grinned from ear to ear, and then, putting it back in his pack, marched off quite as pleased as though he had made a sale.

On the fifth morning, the immaculate water front of Hankow lay before us. As we drew nearer, the appearance of cleanliness persisted. To see anything as habitually neat as the Hankow Bund in anything as habitually untidy as the Chinese Republic pointed to only one conclusion: "Fee, fi, fo, fum; I smell the blood of an Englishman!" Indeed, here were the Foreign Concessions all laid out in building-block patterns as flat as a board. From the shore itself, the building-block effect of the Bund was fortunately somewhat dispelled; but on the whole, the glory of Hankow is not there, but in its new Chinese quarter.

If Shanghai is cosmopolitan, Hankow is metropolitan—with the feeling of a great metropolis in the making. The latter city has been called, "the Chicago of the East"; but the Chicago of the West itself cannot boast of a street with the indescribable *savoir faire* of Taiping Road at night, its myriad electric lights shining through discreet but brilliant ground-glass globes, its conservative jewelry stores that would not be amiss on the Rue de la Paix, and its vanity shops filled with sophisticated lotions and perfumes from all over the civilized world.

A wide, handsome boulevard ran at right angles to Taiping Road. (Was it merely the gentle curve in its length, or was it a certain dignified restraint in this broad, well-paved thoroughfare that recalled the Boulevard Haussmann?) At its eastern end rose a vast, concrete amusement building, the Hsing Sitsong—literally, the Newmarket—holding every variety of entertainment on its roofs and in its halls, from Chinese drama and moving pictures to billiards and singing-girls, with even a secluded library for the world-weary. One performance included a fascinating exhibition of the art of self-defense with dagger, lance, and double-handed sword, the players brandishing their weapons about their heads and bodies with the grace of a martial dance at the Ballet Russe. On leaving the gates after several hours of amusing diversion, I found that the evening's gambol had cost the staggering sum (Columbus Circle please copy) of forty-seven cents!

3

Hankow was by no means the only civic occupant of that particular section of the valley, for not more than two miles away were two other famous cities—Wu-chang, just beyond the Yangtze, and Han-yang, across the Han River, which flows into the Yangtze above Hankow. But I returned from visiting those two elder sisters of Hankow with the very definite feeling that, commercially at least, they were disappointed cities.

Han-yang seems to have suffered most. It must indeed be bitter to see Hankow, which was only a neglected village when she was in her prime, courted by the princes of trade who once bowed before her own gates. Even the huge Han-yang Iron and Steel Works which bear her name are located so far over on the Hankow side of things that the one hundred and eighty-foot chimneys are quite invisible from her walls.

Indeed, as I walked one afternoon along the city's water front, pitiful in its squalor and filth, it seemed to be a place that its gods had forgotten and that had forgotten its gods. A huge Taoist temple—forming the head of Tortoise Hill which lies between Han-yang and Hankow—rose empty and broken above the Yangtze out of a cluster of noisome huts about its base. Another temple a few yards away—incense pots gone, tablets destroyed, beautiful carvings split and blackened—had become a stable for cavalry horses. To see a place where men have worshiped forgotten and falling into ruin may carry with it a certain gentle dignity; but to see a temple, even of pagan gods, where human hearts have looked up with a mysterious trust and hope to something greater than themselves, used as a dumping ground and stable, carried a profound, unanswerable sadness.

Within the walls of the city were other temples, dust-covered and in varying stages of dilapidation. "This is a place of the dead," I thought to myself. But at that moment I paused before a small, well-constructed building opening on an inner court which was surrounded by many rooms and corridors like the refectory of a monastery. Row after row of well-worn desks, shiny from many a youthful wiggle, filled the rooms. Wandering about without meeting anyone, I came again into the outer corridor. On a white tablet near the door was an inscription in Chinese characters, with what appeared to be its English translation beside it:

> Mr. Hai Tze-Chang, (it said), hearing of the Rev. Y. K. Lieo's reconstruction of the Hanyang Christian Middle School, kindly contributed a large sum of money for that purpose. Now, as the work is completed, these few words are, therefore, engraved for memory. 1919 A. D.

"I thought that Han-yang was dead," I mused half-aloud.

"No, my friend," said a pleasant voice behind me, "Han-yang is not dead."

I looked around into the kindly face of a white-haired, spectacled Chinese gentleman of scholarly appearance.

"We of the Christian Middle School," he added with a gentle smile, "think that Han-yang is just beginning to live."

4

Across the two-mile sweep of the Yangtze rise the gray walls of Wu-chang. Having a glorious history to look back upon, and retaining a certain dignity as the present seat of government of Hupeh Province, Wu-chang can no doubt contemplate the successes of Hankow, that *enfant terrible* across the Yangtze, with a broad philosophy. Perhaps she has expected this sort of thing right along. The elder sister in the old tale of the Gebrüder Grimm must occasionally have realized what would happen to Cinderella when the coal-dust and ashes were washed away.

Very gray and very old is Wu-chang, even for China. For nearly three thousand years it has been a city, and most of the time it has been a capital city. Kingdoms have flitted past and imperial dynasties have gone down one after another like houses of cards, but Wu-chang still looks calmly out over the never-returning waters of the Yangtze, as it flows restlessly down toward the sea.

"What is that upon the opposite shore where stood the fishing village of Hankow? What are those great stacks belching flame, and what are those mighty, black cylinders where rock melts into flaming liquid and runs out into the sand in smoking gray bars? And what of that row of stately mansions, and the great iron ships, and that iron road gleaming to the northward?"

"It is a new city, Ancient Friend, a great city—the proud, uprising city of Hankow!"

"Ah well . . . there have been many, many cities. . . ." And the ancient capital goes back to its reverie of the days when the great Sun Chuan stormed its walls, and at last, standing wounded but victorious upon its battlements, proclaimed it the capital of the Kingdom of Wu.

A temple-crowned rock—similar to that in Han-yang—rears high above the walls of Wu-chang. This rock represents the head of a Serpent who lies facing the Tortoise on the opposite shore, while back of Wu-chang, the blue ridges of a line of hills form the back of a sleeping Dragon. These three creatures are said to guard the interests of the three cities, and the sudden rise of Hankow is often attributed to their presence. However, as Hankow is the only city of the three which does not have one of the animals within its own boundaries, their efficacy as municipal Mentors is open to debate.

On arriving in Wu-chang by sampan from across the river, it was at once plain that the temple upon the Serpent's head had degenerated almost as badly as its companion on the head of the Tortoise across the river. Its halls were devoted to tea shops, samshu stalls, and photograph galleries, while the gods themselves had been relegated to four small alcoves in an upper room.

About the wide temple courts, venerable, solemn-eyed geomancers, sitting here and there before small tables, were ready (nay, waiting) to tell the fortunes of the passers-by. Three hundred cash (thirty cents) would bring an abbreviated synopsis of coming events;

four hundred cash would disclose all those events in detail, while five hundred would leave nothing unsaid that might be said. I decided to risk it.

Asking Ah Chow to listen attentively to whatever was related, I sat down at the book-littered table of a large prophet with a benign expression and horn-rimmed spectacles. His entire forecasting outfit consisted of a pair of not immaculate hands equipped with a complete quota of long and razorlike nails which he instantly began to play about my face with all the abandon of an overwrought *maestro di cappello*. Hoping that the prophecy might not include immediate loss of eyesight, I sat still and waited. After a little more preliminary business of feeling my head, thumping my chest and looking at my palms, he seized my left hand and began, his voice booming out through the arches like an assembly bell. In one minute I was the center of a large and eager crowd. In three minutes all egress was blocked by a multitude that hung breathless on every word.

The prediction was in the form of a tabulation of events in short, precise sentences, each sentence beginning with the vociferous preface,

"Yehalla!" What with the humidity of the crowd and that steady bombardment of yehallas in close liaison with the inner ear, I decided after five minutes of it that it was time to depart. With a smile and bow which were meant to convey thanks and finality, I tried to withdraw my hand from the grasp of the prophet, but he only held on the tighter and fairly peppered me with yehallas. Should *he* cheat a foreigner? No-no! Four hundred cash had been paid, and the yehallas were only half finished!

At last (I had begun to have morbid thoughts of knocking him on the head and escaping in the confusion) he relinquished his talonlike grip. We rose moistly and made our way out through that Russian bath of a crowd, which opened in respectful silence before us. For nine minutes by the watch, he had foretold—probably with elaborate detail—just what the future would hold. In spite of a perfect mistrust in anything he might have said, I admitted a certain curiosity as to the surprising wealth of detail.

"What," I asked Ah Chow, "did the fortune teller say?"

"Oh," said Ah Chow, "he say, 'Good luck'!"

CHAPTER V

1

ONE hundred and thirty-five miles below Hankow, a white river steamer, racing down the Yangtze under the combined impetus of its own power and the speed of the current, checked its onward rush, and making a complete circle so that it would again be pointing upstream, came gradually to rest at a floating dock beside the right bank. Beyond the dock lay a tree-shaded riverside street, and beyond the street lay the city of Kiu-kiang. No sooner had the steamer been moored—even before the cables had been made fast and the gangplanks pushed out—than the omnipresent horde of vendors scrambled aboard, but with this marked difference from other vendors along the great river: each of them carried a large basket of chinaware. With utter indifference to the shouting, gesticulating coolies who were removing the baggage of the passengers for Kiu-kiang, they arranged their fragile rice bowls and incense pots row after row upon the narrow decks, until the ship seemed to be no longer a ship but a floating china bazaar. The articles in this astonishing display of ceramics were not of the highest quality, but they pointed to the probability of better things ashore.

After looking at several native hotels along the water front, I went inside the city wall and looked at some more. Without the necessity of any gently qualifying adjectives, they were filthy, so filthy that the presence of a foreign hostelry would have been a sore temptation. But I was spared the ardor of a moral battle. There were no foreign hotels in Kiu-kiang!

Just as we were retracing our steps to the least defiled snuggery along the water, one of the coolies with the baggage was inspired with an idea—it often happens that way in China!— and, following him, we passed along the outer side of the city wall and came at last to a small villa surrounded by arbors and a luxuriant garden full of flowers. Beyond the garden a lake with a temple-bearing island in its center reflected a purple range of mountains in the distance. The villa—formerly the property of an unfortunate mandarin—proved to be a Chinese hotel of the highest quality, and in an excellent upper room facing the Lu-shan mountains across the lake, I gratefully passed several untroubled days and (which is terribly to the point when living Chinese-fashion) untroubled nights.

2

Plainly we had arrived in Kiu-kiang on a gala day. Fire crackers were exploding on all sides. Brilliant red oiled paper lanterns swung in pairs above the doorways, and at short intervals along the street rose temporary booths filled with grotesque paper figures of men and horses. On my asking one of the compradores at the hotel, who spoke a little English, what the ceremony might be, he replied, "To-night, chin-chin the devil."

There were, I knew, ten chief devils each of whom was ruler of one of the ten more or less unpleasant Buddhist hells. I knew that there were many other devils, named or nameless, good or bad, weak or strong, rich or poor, who also had occasionally to be propitiated with offerings of food and paper money to prevent sickness and misfortune. But as for the process of "chin-chinning," I was completely in the dark. This, however, seemed to be the time to get light. At nine o'clock the streets were thronged with citizens, young and old. Lanterns, now alight, flashed in irregular crimson paths above the narrow lanes. The first few paper temples were not yet active. Only a handful of people loitered around them while a long-haired Taoist priest or two lit candles and incense inside their fanciful doorways. But from a distance down the street came the high, cracked note of the gong and the sound of weird music, lifting and falling in dismal nuances. The chin-chinning had begun.

Two heroic paper devils stood fiercely on guard in front of a long, cavernous building on the main street. Inside, ranged along the walls, gilded rickshas, sedan chairs, boats, and temples gleamed in an orgy of color—to say nothing of gorgeous paper equestrians mounted on strange, resplendent dream-creatures, with golden scales and unicorns' horns of silver. On low benches at each side were cups of samshu, tea leaves, lily roots, and other not too expensive delicacies for the devils, who, being short, did their banqueting near the ground. For once, interest in native devils dominated all interest over the foreign kind. I stood entirely unobserved at the edge of the crowd.

In an inner room priests, bowing to the ground, wailed their chant before carved wooden spirit tablets, while on a platform outside, lay-worshipers executed the three deep bows of the kow-tow, dropping a few cash into a box beside them as they rose. Then a new ceremony began. The priests, advancing, slowly circled three times around the platform and passed out of the door in the direction of the lake. On its black surface, hundreds of small lights were moving in a long, curved line toward the opposite shore. The crowd, taking up the paper figures, fell in behind the priests, while torches carried by the novices flickered somberly on the battlements and flared across the yellow faces of the watchers. I, too, followed—as one who goes onward in a dream.

On the shore the procession stopped. Priests, advancing, poured the offerings of food upon the ground. The giant figures with their paper equipages and horsemen were placed on some straw, torches were applied, and amid a thundering crash of drums and gongs, the demons writhed into a mass of red flame. In the glare I looked at the primitive faces about me; and suddenly, this night, like that other which had vibrated to the age-old song of the night watch, seemed to drop like a plummet back through the centuries:

"*I am the King . . . I am Rameses. No man mourneth, no woman weepeth . . . Build thou the great fires. Give offering to Osiris . . .*"

These dignitaries in their straight-falling robes; that high priest in his red mantle, hands poised as in the Egyptian bas-reliefs at Abu-simbel; this crowd of dark, somber-eyed men, who, prompted by dread, were engaged in making burnt-offerings and pouring out libations of wine—surely—*surely* this was a scene from some archaic drama earlier than Æschylus!

Gradually the throng dispersed. One by one, the lights floating over this water which was no other than the Nile, flickered and went out. But in recompense the moon-disc of Isis rose above the hills (were they not the hills of Gizeh?) and sent her soft arrows out over the valley. Or perhaps, after all, it was a later time. In a few moments a galley with deep purple sails and silver oars flashing in the moonlight might separate itself from the black mass of the island, and glide toward that group of cypresses where a Roman consul stood waiting in the shadow . . .

"I think more better you come to hotel," a tired, familiar voice suggested. "This side, plenty robber, plenty tief." Which remark could be relied upon to speed even the most confirmed chronological vagrant back to the realities of our excellent—but not too excellent —twentieth century.

3

The bazaars of Kiu-kiang were filled with the products of the great potteries at King-teh-chen, fifty miles to the southeast—potteries which during a thousand years had presented the best of their fragile wares as tribute to ten dynasties of emperors. China-shops along the water front overflowed into the long parallel street back of it and extended even into the single narrow lane between the city's wall and the Yangtze itself. The connoisseur of old and rare china will probably find a happier hunting-ground in some locality more remote from the potteries, where the ever-flowing current of commerce is less swift. But even in Kiu-kiang, in some dusty, out-of-the-way shop, he may come upon a jar or vase or eggshell cup which calls suddenly and imperiously to him. Let him not say "Ah!" or "Oh!" in reply! One "Ah!" will double the price, two will quadruple it, and any prolonged show of interest will send it on its way in a wild succession of algebraic jumps.

Almost without knowing it, during three days in Kiu-kiang, I accumulated eight pieces of pottery—a blue-black figure of the god Mi La; a glowing, eight-sided red jar (no older than the First Revolution in 1911); an ancient blue vase, probably Ming, "incised to the biscuit"; three ivory-white incense pots; a black jar with green dragons, unclassified but beautiful; and a small tailless lion of evident antiquity, which was salvaged from a heap of dusty junk in a street stall. What, I wondered, was its history? And what was the history of a small glass bottle on the shelf beside it, with a label which read, "Cherry Tooth Paste. Patronized by the Queen"!

Two large gray vases in a bazaar near the river pleaded persistently, with all the allurement of iridescent glaze and flowing line, to be carried bodily away. But it could not be. The baggage had already assumed proportions sufficiently alarming. The original "seven times one are seven" had become "seven times two." It would have been most unfair, I thought, to foist the care of any more bulky breakables upon the narrow though willing shoulders of Ah Chow.

We were to leave Kiu-kiang early the following morning. On returning to the villa at dusk I passed the shining jars with averted head and the virtuous feeling of one who makes a notable sacrifice. But on arriving at the hotel, I found the table piled high with thirty-six large, much-decorated rice bowls, bound together with straw rope. Ah Chow, it seemed, had been making a few purchases of his own!

4

Plainly it was not the custom for a foreigner to travel down the Yangtze on a small boat, for no sooner was I nicely settled on the deck of a tug about to leave for Anking, ninety miles down the river, than a boatload of Chinese river police pulled alongside and requested to see my passport. After its satisfactory perusal, two decrepit but smiling *Greise* (no word fits them like that) were detailed to guard my purse and person as far as Anking. Then—

with certain ominous thuds and bumpings—the engine started, and we were off.

The day was perfect. Overhead a few white clouds scudded across a dome of pure cerulean blue. Eastward before us, the river met and mingled with the sky. To the south, beyond a wide, level valley, rose purple mountains and hills. Northward lay a vast plain, undoubtedly the bed of an ancient ancestor of the Yangtze, its shores dotted here and there with the thatch-roofed, mud-made huts of itinerant gypsies or, as they are called, "Kompo people."

Every year, great numbers of these primitive wanderers from the overcrowded plains north of the Yangtze migrate—whole families at a time—to the neighboring provinces along the river, and usually to the cities, where the prospects of existence seem fairest. Their thatched huts of mud spring up like mushrooms along the city moats, in marshes, on rocky hillsides or among ruins—anywhere, in fact, where mud and straw will hold together without legal or physical interference. Great numbers of these people who can find no building space on land live on boats and gradually become identified with the "boat people." The men do any work that may be at hand, such as pulling rickshas, repairing shoes, and pushing wheelbarrows, while their wives become "sew-sew women" and sit at the street corners putting on patches for homeless coolies. Almost they appear to be of an older, simpler race than the populace of the cities. And yet the same uncomplaining acceptance of their lot proves that they are all Chinese.

5

Toward evening mountains appeared to the north marshaling the clouds into long parallel ranks about them, while the sun sent its last light in pale banners across the valley. Then, with the delicate gradations of an old Chinese painting, the warm color faded from the sky, and left the river veiled in translucent blue. So came dusk, and out of the dusk shone the lights of Anking. And just then—the engine broke!

The engineer and his assistants immediately busied themselves with repairs. Unscrewing a large iron plate from the boiler's side, they plugged some very obvious holes underneath with bits of rag, clapped on the plate and pulled a lever. But the engine did not go.

Taking off the plate again, they rubbed the rags with graphite, rebolted the plate, and pulled the lever a second time. Escaping steam took a higher pitch, and the two old guardsmen who were to protect my life and money, moved to a place where, in case of trouble, they would be able to fill at least half of their obligation with as sound bodies as possible. As the tug was well out in the current and drifting rapidly downstream, it was plain that we were about to break the old Chinese maxim which says, "Enter the inn before dark." But just as we were parallel with the city, the engine started as suddenly as it had stopped and the tug made for the jetty which was heavily guarded with soldiers.

The city was under martial law. A week earlier bands of Chinese infantry, many of whom had received no pay in six months, had expressed their disapproval by looting a number of shops all over Anking—after which they had been promptly outlawed. Since the brigands were paying high prices with their purloined money for contraband arms and ammunition, introductions were the order. But even without a passport it is probable that a small white card with a foreign name—any name—engraved thereon would have been sufficient means of "identification." In China a foreign card seems always to exert a sort of hypnotic influence of persuasion even when other more logical means fail.

Darkness had indeed overtaken the city. But at last an inn was found—a very small inn with red-tiled floor, square teakwood furniture, and a large circular doorway with a legend of cheerful greeting at the top. The host, a stout gentleman in slippers and trousers only, rose and invited inspection of the available rooms. The inn had five rooms in all, including a *chambre de luxe* in a sort of shedlike addition over the back. Though the *chambre* would have suffered badly in comparison with any self-respecting vegetable cellar, it appeared to be farthest from the earth and things earthy, so I took it. The choice was not entirely happy, for the odors of the kitchen directly below rose pungently on high, reminding one of the good old days in Merrie England when prisoners were starved to death in cells above the kitchens, dejectedly sniffing the fragrance of little roast pigs with apples in their mouths.

But it soon became apparent that no prisoner in the *chambre de luxe* would have lingered on, to die of hunger, for the kitchen fuel, which consisted of briquettes of coal dust and dry mud, gave off such noxious, deadly fumes that strangulation must shortly have ensued. On the other hand, the room, because of its state of atmosphere, was free as the moon itself from all trace of animal life, so that by avoiding it at meal times and by rising early, an equitable balance of comfort was maintained.

Anking was a thoroughly Chinese city. Of its five hundred thousand inhabitants only twenty were foreigners. When a white man passed along the streets, the little boys would cough with great noise and demonstration to attract his attention so they could see the color of his eyes. (It is an impressive commentary on early foreign activities in China that most Chinese devils have blue eyes and red beards.) No rows of foreign buildings broke the city's water front into hard, uncomprising building-block sections as in Hankow. And yet in some peculiar way foreign influence had filtered in, more than in some of the treaty ports with their foreign settlements; much of the beef for sale in the butcher shops was inclosed in

Mine host at Anking makes his reckoning. The characters above the circular doorway mean that the inn is centrally located—and good.

fly-proof screens, and small cakes and pastries were displayed under glass.

To ride in one of Anking's iron-rimmed rickshas was to receive a sensation long to be remembered. In Shanghai, the ricksha coolies put down their heads and traveled at break-neck speed. In Hankow, they indulged in a sort of dog trot. In Anking, very fortunately, they walked, for its streets, being somewhat rolling, were paved at frequent intervals with low stone steps. On the steamship *Nanking* there had been a gentleman who at one time had traveled for four months in a springless oxcart from eastern Manchuria across the steppes of Thibet to the Turkestan frontier. Even when he told about it I had thought him something of a martyr; but after I had traveled for two hours in a springless ricksha over the steps of Anking his canonization was complete.

6

Just as Paris is dominated by the Eiffel Tower and Genoa by the Lanterne, so Anking is recognizable by its great pagoda, the Chen Teng ("Stirred by the wind"), which stands beyond the city's east gate. There is a superstition in the locality—probably because three of Anking's gates are washed by the Yangtze —that the city is not built upon a solid base, but that the ground it rests on is only moored to the shore like a boat. Two huge anchors, embedded in the soil near the pagoda, prevent the city from floating down the river. To carry the imagery still further, the pagoda is pointed out as the mast. Beneath, there is buried a large oar of teak, which, together with the anchors, has succeeded up to the present time in holding the city in a stable and secure position.

Coming out of the pagoda I saw an old woman, who was carrying an infant, put her hand over the baby's eyes so that it might not suffer any evil results from being looked at by a foreigner! But that type of superstition is fast disappearing. Foreigners are permitting themselves to be understood. And—I say it gladly—Americans seem to have taken the lead. Perhaps the friendly attitude toward us is partly due to our prompt decision to use the American share of the Boxer Indemnity to further Chinese education, or to other more recent policy on the part of the State Department. Whatever the cause, I can at least report the result. Even in the most isolated city along the lower Yangtze, it was only necessary to say "Maquan" (American), to bring a distinctly friendly look into those half-apprehensive faces, with smiles quite different in character from the rubbery face-stretchings of Swiss innkeepers in the vicinity of Interlaken. Many a cup of tea was given, and when the cup was lacking, many a teapot was offered so that one might drink directly from the spout. And what greater proof of friendliness could there be on the part of a host—or a guest—than that?

7

Close beside the north wall of Anking was a large American hospital. Its wards for men, women, and children were filled to capacity with Chinese patients who would carry away with them at least a transient impression of sanitation and a growing confidence in foreign medicine. Recently a maniac wielding an ax wounded nineteen Chinese in the streets of Anking. Fourteen of the wounded came to the foreign hospital for treatment.

It took a long time to establish such confidence. The great initial fear of the white man's hospital seemed to lie in the widely credited belief that the doctors would "make

Chinee fella go asleep; after, cut off leg, arm, ear." Such a thought is very distressing to the Chinese, who believe that only those mortals with a complete set of bones can enjoy perfect felicity after death. Before the hospital at Anking could unpack the skeleton which was to be used for the instruction of its nurses it was necessary for the doctor in charge to take oath before the municipal authorities that none of the bones were Chinese; upon which a handsome certificate stating that fact and bearing the vice-regal seal was hung in the reception room where all who cared to look might see. But the story of Zing, an old one-legged coolie who works in the hospital's drying-room, is even a more graphic portrayal of love of limb than the certificate in the reception room.

Some twenty years ago, when the hospital was new, the man Zing appeared one day with a leg that badly needed amputation. "The patient consented." During his convalescence, he made himself so useful about the grounds and garden that later he was added to the force. A short time after, a young boy was brought in for a trouble similar to Zing's. His leg was also amputated, and in good season he was sent home. The following year, the relatives of the boy returned to the hospital. He had died of cholera, they explained, and one more leg was necessary to put him commendably to rest. During the year, the hospital had been rebuilt on a larger scale in a different part of the compound, and no one had any idea where the missing limb was buried. The relatives, however, with much weeping (and some gnashing of teeth, I understand), demanded one human leg, complete in all its articulations.

At last, after great effort, a set of leg bones was unearthed from somewhere, and presented with proper ceremony to the gratified relatives. But just as they were leaving the compound, Zing, the coolie, sprang dramatically from the kitchen-house and claimed the bones for his own. "If you never b'lieve him b'long myside, makee measure it!" he said.

Measurements were taken, and the bones were found exactly to match those of Zing's other leg! The doctor in charge, quite at his wits' end, sent down the river to Shanghai for an artificial limb, which on arriving was presented to the bereaved relatives with even more ceremony than before. They retired, perfectly satisfied. But since that day, all patients who undergo amputations in the hospital at Anking carry the glistening framework of their unattached members with them when they go; while the coolie, Zing, not taking any chances of hobbling about in the Hereafter, sleeps at night with his treasured keepsake in a well-made box under his bed.

Anking, aside from being a typically Chinese city, is not particularly rich in matters of interest; so, after persuading the landlord of the inn to sit for a sketch within his circular doorway, I continued down the river—one hundred and sixty miles down the river—to the classical city of Nanking.

CHAPTER VI

1

ON the three-mile drive from the Yangtze to the center of the city of Nanking, it was plain that if the city had never been conquered by foreigners, as the native driver told us, its outskirts at least had fallen under the hand of foreign builders. (What god of discord and wrath, I wonder, directs the designing of foreign consulates in China!) But the situation was presently saved by a formidable, antique drum-tower which reared its huge bulk defiantly across the road. A party of American senators had recently been entertained in Nanking for thirty-five hours, at a cost to the Chinese government of one thousand dollars an hour, and as a result, the drum-tower was fuming under a heavy, feverish-looking coat of red paint—a symbol which might have had aspects of humor to anyone who was not engaged in searching for such a dodo bird as a cleanly Nanking hotel. At last, in desperation, the baggage was poured into a small receptacle of a lodging which Ah Chow assured me was "too clean"—and the city lay before me.

2

Nanking is planned on a scale that is worthy of its imperial history. Its splendid fourteenth-century wall, rising in places to a height of fifty feet, sweeps in giant curves around a circumference of almost thirty miles. Let no enthusiastic visitor with limited time attempt to see Nanking on foot. Its places of interest lie at great and involved distances from one another. But they may not be neglected, for the history of Nanking is vividly intermingled with the history of China itself.

In the days when Peking was only a small town on a precarious frontier, Nanking was the capital and metropolis of all China, vying in splendor with the proudest capitals of Europe. Even as the driver said, no foreign invader, whether Mongol or Manchu or European, has ever held the city. Between the fourth and seventh centuries, six dynasties flourished within its walls. In 1368 the Ming dynasty, having succeeded in wresting the throne from the degenerate successors of Kublai Khan, set up its first government there. Again, in 1853, it became the stronghold of the mighty Taiping

RIVER CITIES 111

Rebellion, which lasted fifteen years and shook the empire to its foundations. During those terrible years, probably *three times as many lives were lost* as in the Great War in Europe! After a rapid and triumphant campaign down the Yangtze Valley, the Taiping leader, who at one time or another had absorbed some of the tenets of Christianity, captured the city and made it his capital, freeing the slaves, prohibiting prevalent vices—including foot-binding—and establishing a kingdom which he called the "Kingdom of the Great Peace." The Ten Commandments were expounded as Divine Law and adapted to current conditions by making the seventh read, "Thou shalt not commit adultery nor smoke opium."

But the leader of the revolt, like so many of the world's men of action, was not a statesman. With China in his hands, he could not hold it. Nanking was surrounded with one hundred and thirty-eight forts, and after a seven months' siege of unspeakable horror, the walls were mined and the garrison slaughtered.

The Taipings failed, but they so shattered the power of the Manchus that when the year 1911 ushered in a new revolution with the old war cry, "China for the Chinese," the three-hundred-and-sixty-year-old dynasty crumbled to earth with very little of the rending and thunder which usually has accompanied similar upheavals. Nanking, being as usual the provisional capital of the new republic, was again the scene of bloodshed. The pigtail, that badge of servitude under the Manchus, at once became an important issue. When the Republican forces occupied the city, they seized as many inhabitants as possible and cut off the hated symbol of bondage close to the head. Later on the Imperial troops captured the city, apprehended the same queueless citizens, and holding such defection to be revolutionary, removed the head itself. At last, prompted by a strong desire for conservation of their species, the citizen body bought a large consignment of foreign caps. Rolling their queues tight about their heads, they pulled the caps well down over their ears and went their way. This incognito quite satisfied the finally victorious Republicans, who were probably beginning to see that their principles had at last penetrated well below the hair. The policy of leniency continues, and to-day, the preponderating masses of China's citizens, wear—and will continue to wear—their "hair in a braid."

3

In order to orient myself within the thirty-mile circumference of the city, I climbed the Pe-chi-ko, a temple upon a hill near the center of the north wall. Far to the south, the open, desolate site of the old Ming palace was visible. To the northwest rose the smoke of Nanking's busy suburb on the Yangtze. Stretching away from the foot of the hill to the west lay the city itself, dotted with temples, foreign churches, primary schools, high schools, military schools, technical schools, and the clustering buildings of two universities. The wells of Nanking were inclined to be brackish. Not so the waters of its Pierian springs! They had gone through the filtering processes of two civilizations, and there was unlimited opportunity for drinking deeply. Even the Y. M. C. A. advertised the services of ten teachers in English!

East of Pe-chi-ko, on a somewhat lower hill, stood another temple, its outer stairs built of long, flintlike gray bricks, the manufacture of which is now a forgotten industry. Extreme care had been taken in their making, and each bore the name and city of the long-departed donor, in raised characters on its surface. The neighborhood—an execution ground in ancient days—was formerly infested with the wandering souls of criminals and was the nightly resort of specters and ghosts; an altogether disreputable place from a psychic point of view. As an antidote, a house had been built near at hand by the first Ming emperor where offerings were made "to the friendless dead." These ceremonies, together with the presence of the two temples in the vicinity, had either propitiated the ghosts or frightened them away. On questioning the caretaker, I found that he had seen only seven ghosts in the last ten years, a negligible total in the light of recent figures from other lands!

On the other side of the city was a still more potent example of progress—the passing of the old-time examination booths. Along a canal had stood row after row of narrow, gray-brick cells, each about four feet wide by six feet long, containing nothing but a rude table and a bench on which the scholar who was to occupy the cell might sleep. At certain times during the year, aspiring men of any age or rank, who had been successful in the smaller governmental examinations in the outlying towns, competed here for "the honorable grade of Chu-jen," the winning of which led to candidacy for the highest examination in Peking. The final test of wisdom took place in the presence of the Emperor and consisted in answering a question put by the monarch himself. A successful candidate might be quite ignorant of matters of the day, might never before have been outside of his native town, and yet, if he could write a more transcendent commentary than his fellows on a few lines from Confucius, he might become the governor of a million men.

But China—as has been said by everyone east of the one hundred and forty-third meridian (and nearly everyone west of it)—is awakening. The educational system has been renovated, and the ground so long enclosed by those gray, honeycombed walls has been sold to the highest bidder.

Scrambling over several piles of brick, I approached the few remaining rows of cells, which stood silent and forlorn in the center of a group of large, brilliantly lighted tea houses going up around them. I had read a number of descriptions of Chinese examination booths, and had always pictured each aspirant as working with bursting head in the stifling, feverish atmosphere of an air-tight kennel lighted by a single candle. So it was with pleasure and surprise that I found the cells to have only three walls. The fourth side was open to the air! Of course it was just possible that each cell had at one time a tight-fitting wooden back, which in the course of the demolition had been removed. But it was better as it was! As I climbed back over the bricks and debris, I decided that I, for one, would never inquire about it. The cramped quarters and the narrow sleeping-boards of the candidates must have been bad enough. In my own mind at least, they should not suffer for want of light and air.

4

There was another famous institution in the vicinity—the flower boats on the Chin-kwai River at the southern end of the city. To dine beside the Chin-kwai and watch the stately passage along the stream of the dozens of gaily decorated boats—each cabin shining in the darkness like a small illuminated stage on which strutted some Chinese Don Juan or Carmen, or which carried Father and Mother Tyl and the rest of the family (including the Bluebird) for a pleasant, wholesome outing—was an interesting and varied pageant of Chinese life not to be paralleled in any other Yangtze city.

At the west wall not far from the flower boats stood the four rounded arches of the formidable west gate which many times in the past had been the scene of stubborn conflict. As a bulwark against modern aggression, the gate ranks with that now obsolete Chinese war council, the Ping-poo. Not more than sixty years ago the Ping-poo was still sending out instructions to the Chinese infantry to make faces in order to frighten the enemy! Such was the potency of that dread body's august name that a battalion of loyal troops is said to have dispersed a large army of rebels by merely making faces and snapping out in unison the horrid name "Ping-poo"—(but I cannot vouch for *that!*)

Near the wall was a large Confucian temple, the Tsau-lien-kung. As the temple gate was locked, it was necessary to go up a small lane to find the gateman. Half way up the lane a large crowd had gathered around an open doorway; and out of the doorway came the clatter of a human tongue going at a speed which gave the grotesque and somewhat monstrous impression that the tongue had got control and was actually running away. Before we came within thirty yards, I understood what was happening. Someone was engaged in the time-honored custom of "saving the face."

This particular type of face-saving is usually restricted to women. When a woman of the humbler classes feels that she has a sufficient grievance, she will wait until she reaches the "end of her rope" and then go to some public or semipublic place where, for one, two or three hours, she will tell the world all about it.

Out of that wild chaos of lingual dots and dashes Ah Chow managed to salvage a few stray waifs of thought. The woman, it seemed, was not being appreciated. Her husband had died years before, and instead of marrying again she had remained a widow, thereby upholding all that was best in Chinese custom. She was not asking anyone to build her a *pai-lu* (arch), but she just wanted people to know what was what. She had had a suitor, she said. There wasn't any doubt about that —a very good suitor whose intentions had been of the best—a dark, handsome man from Ningpo, with sufficient money too. But she had not married him; and so he had died! (At this point there was a short pause in order that the spectators might draw, if they chose, a logical, if somewhat sentimental, conclusion as to cause and effect.) And now, after all that, she was not being appreciated. She not only embroidered all day but cooked the meals for her sister's family without getting a word of thanks. While she didn't want any praise, she *did* want them to remember this . . .

Just then the gateman came with the key and opened a side gate of the temple. The inner court brought a swift contrast of silence and wide space. Here were double rows of slender, sky-pointing cypresses, a bronze bell supported by aged, teakwood lions with curling manes carved evenly as in the sculpture of archaic Greece, and a smooth-tiled roof glowing with the vibrant colors of a Phœnician tear vase. The outer court—by way of further contrast—had been converted into a model military barracks. In its center, squad drill, including a slow "goose-step" (probably imported from Germany via Japan), was being carried on with vigor and precision. Small covered alcoves around the sides had been converted into class rooms in which sat many soldiers, who, with wrinkled brows and vertical brushes held upright in unresponding fingers, were trying to form a few of the forty thousand characters which comprise the written language. On going a little closer, I saw something which will always, I think, put me more at ease in the presence of a Chinese fighting man. Five of those doughty warriors—sitting all in a row—were giving their wobbling fingers moral support by going through the same painstaking motions with the ends of their tongues!

In what kindly and humorous ways the genial angel of everyday things has bound us all together!

5

In China the palaces of its kings are either in repair or in dust, for each succeeding dynasty seemed always to satisfy its passing ambition for reform by blotting out every vestige of the predecessor's glory.

Passing through a gateway near Nanking's busiest street, I came, not into the heart of the city but into a wilderness where the ancient Imperial City of the first of the Ming emperors had stood. Here was utter prostration. In all the vast inclosure, hardly one brick rested upon another. Like the Coliseum and the Acropolis, it had furnished building material for countless years to the surrounding countryside.

Isolated coolie huts had sprung up here and there, and fields of corn, waist-high, served somewhat to soften the outlines of its bitter desolation. From the center of that broken area rose three large buttresses which had marked the boundaries of "The Red Forbidden City," the magnificent palace of the "Sun-born Emperor." And what of all that magnificence now? Five narrow footbridges over a dried-up canal, a small museum containing a few pitiful ornaments and tiles, a broken monument to an old scholar—and that was all! Corrosion, *rigor mortis,* the End. And yet—as always—out of that necrosis, that finality, rose the whispered, hopeful questionings of a new beginning—the voices of children playing among the ruins; the song of the coolies from the neighboring fields; the wind rustling down the lanes of growing corn . . .

6

Out through the city's eastern gate, three miles beyond the Ming palace rose a vast, tree-covered mound—the tomb of Tai-tsin, the founder of the Ming dynasty. Heroic stone figures of men and horses marked the way to the burial hill, while along a smaller road to the east, a procession of great carved elephants, ponderous lions, massive horses, and certain large unidentified animals of ample girth, led to a colonnade in which a mammoth stone tortoise carried uncomplainingly upon its back an obelisk covered with royal inscriptions.

Tai-tsin must have been a monarch of tremendous force. A fragment of a portrait in the museum of the Red Forbidden City showed the profile of a remarkable, elongated face terminating in a jawbone beside which the most lantern-jawed scion of the Hapsburgs would appear practically chinless. The Mings were pleased to find in themselves certain resemblances, facial and otherwise, to the pig; but it should immediately be stated that the social standing of the pig in *vieux* Cathay was unchallenged, and that even to-day, the Chinese word for "home" is made by placing the character for "pig" under the character for "roof."

Soon after the death of Tai-tsin the seat of government was transferred to Peking on the north, where the greatest danger to the Empire lay. And from that time onward the glory of Nanking has waned. To-day, the population of the city has dwindled to one hundred and fifty thousand—a mere fraction of its former strength. Its one-time world-famous trade in silks and damasks no longer holds a place of prominence. Imports are vastly greater than exports—a sad plight for an export city—and its shops are full of machine-made sateens and other foreign materials which sell for lower prices than the silks from its own hand looms. Its weavers—the most industrious and skillful workmen in the world—start their looms at dawn, often weaving until midnight, but the demand for handmade silks is lessening, and the cities farthest from the home of the silkworm suffer first. The splendid "Nankeen" silks, which lasted for generations in the days when generations wanted them to last, will soon be only a memory.

Apropos of that, an American gentleman returning home after several days' absence and embracing his Fair Lady with a discreet but affectionate hug (as he had been taught), was greeted with, "Oh, don't tear my waist!"

"Very well, Delilah," he answered, swelling

up his chest and stroking back his locks in a fierce, Samsonian manner.

"No, *that* isn't it," she said; "but silk nowadays is simply *miserable!* I think I'll wear sackcloth. (That reminds me, dear, will you take out the ashes?)"

But, Fair Lady, what under the starry canopy would you do with a silk dress that lasted twenty years, as your great-grandmother's did? Just *imagine* it! And to be strictly honest, what blame-shifting Adam's son of us would want you to wear a dress that lasted for twenty years? *Tempora* and *mores* again; building, changing, destroying, rebuilding . . . Sometimes, it would seem that we, like those other people of a more ancient China, are selling our reliable old lamps for new ones which perhaps give a more brilliant light, but which may at any moment go out and leave us in darkness. Ah well . . . whatever our own troubles, may we be prepared to meet them like the weavers of Nanking—with the armor of work well done, and a sturdy, unconquerable philosophy.

THE ISLAND OF BUDDHA

CHAPTER VII

1

*My ears have heard the chant of swift rain
   falling,
The peal of temple bells on a far breeze,
The dash of sea-waves, and the wild birds
   calling
   From your wild headlands down the wast-
   ing seas . . .*

THE host of the inn at Kiu-kiang had told compellingly of a strange island somewhere beyond the China coast—an island of high crags and deep valleys among which lay seventy Buddhist monasteries and temples. *Seventy?* That settled it!

Ah Chow, faithful, kindly soul, had entered into every previous plan with great good will. He had endured without complaint the grilling of continuous summer travel in central China and had explained all matters to the best of his broken English. But when I said that I wanted to go to the island of Puto-shan he received that announcement with manifest hesitation.

"Somebody say, Puto very hot," he said. "Have got big hill. If go up, never can come down same day. Somebody say, have got plenty big snake; on table, in bed. If man hurt snake, priest make knock man down. Sometime, foreign man go there; drink the whiskey, make the big shout. Somebody say, priest never like to see him—"

But Ah Chow, without knowing it, was adding just the right amount of stimulus to carry the *Ausflug* triumphantly on its way. It was necessary to take a steamer from Nanking down the coast to the port of Ningpo. This time, I knew what to expect—the small cabin, the narrow decks lined with "space passengers," the ticket brigade composed of eight or ten men (all watching each other, and each on the lookout for a little extra cumshaw), the hawkers, the steaming bowls of rice—all the absorbing matters that went to make up the accelerated motion-picture of native steamboat travel.

Ningpo was the ancestral port of those "boats with eyes" which had sailed up over the horizon, with their friendly welcome from Shanghai, several months earlier. Here they were "at home"—small junks with eyes like

After being stroked with straws until they become "plenty mad," two crickets are placed in a small bowl where they bump each other—head on—until one or the other is vanquished. The winner is hailed with cheers.

THE ISLAND OF BUDDHA

croquet balls, middle-sized junks with optics the size of bowling balls, ocean junks with bulging eyes three feet across—rough lads, these round-orbed sea-gamins, but merry fellows with a keen sense of humor. When the weather was a little heavy, half the time the eyes would be submerged, but finally when they peered out at one for an instant above the surface of the water they seemed to twinkle with a sort of suppressed humor just as much as to say: "Between you and me, this eye business is a joke. But *I* certainly am not the one to give it away if you don't." And then they would take a big breath and plunge under the waves again.

Many of the streets of Ningpo could easily be measured by the span of a man's arms. The main street, however, was wide even for a Chinese city—although a ten-ton truck would have had its paint badly scraped driving through. The city's narrow canals, filled with green, heavy-looking water, were even less passable for houseboats than those of Hang-chow, and the bridges were only just high enough to allow the small, local sampans—equipped with eyes, of course—to nose their way along in a sort of near-sighted, quizzical manner. The water in the Ningpo canals was enough to make anyone quizzical . . .

2

A small steamer left Ningpo at daybreak for the island of Puto-shan. Peddlers, eternally vigilant, were as usual crying their wares—this time a gala assortment of yellow watermelons, gongs, prayer beads, incense, Florida water, and rat-traps. Ningpo lay thirteen miles up its river much after the manner of Shanghai. On passing several forts at the river's mouth, which had been constructed by German engineers for the Manchus, one half expected to see the long waves of the Pacific come thundering in upon the beach. But the boat plunged into a perfect labyrinth of green, hill-covered islands which were separated by narrow straits of swirling, treacherous water, waveless but filled with eddies.

Seventy years ago the English tentatively occupied a few of these islands (the Chousan Archipelago) but abandoned them after a year or two in favor of Hongkong—stopping long enough, however, to introduce that plant which Mr. William Beebe, writing in the *Atlantic Monthly,* might without arrogance classify as the *Solanum tuberosum,* but which I, alas!

THE ISLAND OF BUDDHA

must call the Irish potato. Many of the hills were terraced like those of the Italian lake country. On others the potato patches followed the irregularities of the ground, making great natural arabesques in viridian green across the emerald of the hillsides.

Upon the boat itself the majority of passengers were either gray-clad Buddhist priests or lay pilgrims who, with laughter on their lips and holiday attire on their persons, were on their way to visit the temples and monasteries of the sacred island. Watching them, one's thoughts carried unerringly back to the story of that other jovial, primitive company which once in the long-ago rode merrily in the spring sunlight over the Southwark meadows toward Canterbury. For here beyond doubt were the convivial miller, the mendicant friar, the clerk, the host, the monk, the man of law,

> "Well nyne and twenty in a compaignye
> Of sondry folk by aventure y-falle
> In felawshipe. . . ."

"each with his own disposition, face, costume, turn of speech, little significant actions," for nowhere more quickly than in China itself comes the negation of the statement that "all

Chinese look alike." Suddenly—a surprising anachronism in that strictly Oriental gathering—I saw near me at the rail a magnificent red beard under a large white sun-helmet, and below it, the close-fitting black cassock of the Mission Catholique. A pair of friendly blue eyes looked out at me from beneath the sun-helmet. Their owner was graciously waiting for me to speak.

"Bon jour, mon père," I said (after the school of Stratford-atte-bowe, or worse), "je suis heureux—"

"Never mind," he interrupted with a twinkle in his eye as he heartily held out his hand. "You don't have to do that. I'm Irish!"

For three pleasant hours before reaching the island fishing-town of Sin-ko-men which was his parish, we talked of many things—except the thing I should most like to have known: how an Irish priest, certainly not over twenty-five, came to be buried in the middle of China in a French mission. He got off at Sin-ko-men and as the boat passed on toward Puto-shan, I saw his black-robed figure waving a genial farewell from the white gateway of the small Residence on the hillside above the peaked roofs of the village.

3

In the meantime Ah Chow, being of a practical mind, had made certain inquiries about the manner of living on the sacred island. Among others he had met a Buddhist secretarial monk who said that accommodations might possibly be found at his own temple, half a mile inland. The steamer did not moor directly at the small pier, but dropped anchor a few hundred yards from the island; whereupon a perfect frenzy of boats attached themselves to her sides, some empty except for the crew, some carrying passengers for the steamer's return trip—all bearing a wild rabble of boatmen who filled the air with staccato comments on the speed and excellence of their boats, or begged, with groans and entreaties almost Sicilian in their emotional energy, for a little more cumshaw.

Running the gauntlet of swinging booms and waving oars, we arrived on shore. Ah Chow remained at the pier while I went forward with the Buddhist secretary. The way led through a wide cleft in the hills into the heart of the island. On either side, grassy hill-slopes rose to rugged, rock-strewn summits hundreds of feet above. Here and there among towering gray cliffs, or half-hidden in small valleys, shone the white walls of temples and monasteries. Below us, in a valley filled with the foliage of great trees, glistened a tiled temple-roof of imperial yellow—the sacred color of the Manchu emperors. Skirting the temple, we passed upward on the other side of the valley through a hillside village, where stone images, beads, amulets, and other pilgrim gear were for sale. Beyond the village the road narrowed into a winding, high walled lane. Several flights of rugged stone steps led through a twilight of old trees and huge, moss-covered boulders carved with inscriptions. And so we came at last to our destination—the Temple of the Grotto.

The court was small, and the shrine with its gilded gods was on the second floor among the branches of trees. Here was an atmosphere of quiet—serene and grateful after those strenuous days on the Yangtze. Into the high chamber which was to be mine, the fresh breeze of the sea swept through the open window under the temple eaves; and there, three hundred feet below, was the sea itself, deep blue between rocky promontories. A broad band of shining breakers—strong with the strength of their five-thousand-mile sweep—crashed on a strip of silver beach. I checked the Chinese character in my notebook which meant "wanted," and handed it to the secretary.

4

The personnel of the Temple of the Grotto consisted of an abbot or *Chee Foo,* his brother (a business man of forty-five years who was going through his novitiate), four elderly priests, the secretary, and several coolies who carried the sedan chairs and did the cooking. This, almost needless to say, was the first Buddhist temple in which I had ever lived; while I was the first white guest at the temple during the whole of its three hundred years. The monks on passing me in the corridors invariably bowed with a grave courtesy and greeted me with their age-old salutation, *"O mi do vah,"* ("Peace be with you"), to which I would reply with a short but well-meant *"Sow ah!"* ("Good day"), hoping in the meantime that they would not think I was calling them anything as unpleasant as it sounded. One old monk who three years before had been an officer in the Chinese army, was unable to forget his earlier training and always welcomed me with a humorous combination of pagan blessing and military salute. In spite of his very pious manner I always imagined that the old fellow had retired from the army with a speed which gave his retirement the nature of a sudden rout. It was no secret that he had changed his name on one or two previous occasions.

The monasteries and temples are still "cities of refuge" for numbers of men who, having gone well beyond the law, find shelter in these sanctuaries, have the twelve sacred spots burned on their heads, and become priests. Other postulants—for example, the Chee Foo's brother, who was married and had a wife and several children in Hang-chow—appear merely to be forsaking the cares (and duties) of the world for a life of ease; while others, usually young men and boys, impelled by high religious motives, join the various orders and become the spiritual support of Chinese Buddhism.

There were two other guests at the Temple of the Grotto. One, a maker of clocks and watches from Ningpo, was on his annual trip to the island repairing the monastic timepieces. The sea air seemed to work swift havoc among their wheels and weights, for the watchmaker would often come back at night with five or

THE ISLAND OF BUDDHA 137

six dollars as his day's earnings. And yet he worked for two hours on my own watch which had been ailing, taking it completely apart, cleaning it and assembling it—for twenty cents! But then, there were other mysteries in China connected with the watchmakers' trade. Six hundred miles up the Yangtze, I had found American Ingersoll watches for sale at lower prices than in the United States!

The third guest was a pathetic little old man who was trying to sell ginseng, that almost useless root which is so highly venerated by the Chinese for its alleged medicinal qualities. Either the genuineness of his stock was doubtful or the pilgrims were too busy to buy, for during the three days of his stay, he sold only one small, hairy root, and that was to Ah Chow, who, I think, bought it purely out of compassion.

Twice during each twenty-four hours sacred rites were held to Quan Yin, the Chinese Goddess of Mercy and patroness of the island, in each of the seventy or more temples and monasteries. On the night of my arrival, the temple bell, just below my room, had boomed out in the darkness at three A. M. This was followed by an hour of low rhythmic chanting accompanied by the light pounding of a "wooden fish" and punctuated at intervals by the note of a small, clear bell. Every morning at three the ceremony was repeated; but instead of being a disturbance it brought the pleasant, semiconscious assurance that there were still to be several hours of delightful slumber before the coming of dawn.

Dawn brought breakfast. Breakfast consisted of bamboo shoots, wild cabbage, brown rice, and another comestible which at first sight looked as nearly as possible like toasted marshmallows in a thin, brownish gravy.

"What is that?" I asked.

"That?" said Ah Chow, "that—*bean curd!*"

I shied at the word, for the memory of a certain unsavory dish at the Oriental Hotel was still upon me, and the thought of bean curd in any guise left me strangely cold. But at last I tasted it, finding it decidedly edible. Evidently, there was bean curd and bean curd. And, fortunately; for during several weeks upon the island it appeared in a variety of forms—sometimes cut into cubes, sometimes shredded, sometimes in thin, clothlike squares which were tied into knots and bore upon their surface the impression of the cloths between which they had been pressed. These, together with soy beans, seaweed soup, potatoes, pickled moss, and tea, completed the menu. And the menu was *table d'hôte*. Breakfast, luncheon and dinner were all alike—meat was taboo and eggs were not to be found on the island. Bread, butter, milk, coffee? "Thin airy shoals of visionary ghosts!" It did not require a profound mental effort or the natural qualities of a Sherlock Holmes to understand just why Ah Chow had not been more enthusiastic over the prospect of coming to Puto-shan!

5

But the temples and the monasteries were there—seventy of them as the host of the inn at Kiu-kiang had said. The island was continually thronged with pilgrims, and the sound of temple bells and the sea mingled by day and by night in an exalted harmony. The imperial, yellow-roofed Weng-sin-sz, of which I had caught a glimpse on the first day in Puto-shan, will always remain in my memory as the perfect Buddhist temple—chaste, æsthetic, complete. From its broad, stone-rimmed pool to the sanctum of the high priest on the rising hillside beyond its three wide courts, no element of its perfectness was lacking. Hours at a time I lingered about the ancient courtyards painting a bridge here, or a gateway there, and watching the vast accumulated pageantry of modern Buddhism. Sometimes—delightful sin!—I engaged myself in the pleasant occupation of doing nothing at all.

By day the terraces were thronged with pilgrims whose chair-coolies filled the outer court, but at the hour of sunset it was usually quite empty. Then, after sending away my paints and canvas, I would go a little distance down the road, and turning, come back slowly toward the outer gate. In the valley was no sound of the sea to disturb its mood of profound contemplation. Two bridges spanned the great mirroring pool which lay before the wall. The Lion Bridge—so named because of fifty stone lions along the balustrades—rose gracefully in a high white arch over its reflected curve in the water below. The second bridge led straight across the pool only a few feet above the lotus leaves, and carried on its central span an orange-hued shrine where pilgrims might rest before entering the temple. Passing through the outer gate, one entered a different world. Golden tiles glowing under the

Central China is by no means treeless. The shadow-patterns of foliage against white walls leave an ineffaceable memory.

last shafts of the sun, flamed half-hidden amid the dark foliage of mighty trees. Indigo shadows, moving with splendid majesty—like minute hands of the day—passed slowly across courtyards where ancient bronze braziers exhaled sinuous lines of blue, curling incense against sun-flecked walls.

Here indeed was beauty. Yet why, in its presence, should there come, as always, that strange exultation so much like pain? And why at such times should the heart rise up and demand imperiously to speak when the lips are so strangely mute? If only we might speak *then!*

Beyond the court gleamed dusky, colorful interiors—dim corridors where immobile rows of great golden gods and lohans sat in their perpetual twilight. Countless gray-robed priests passed in solemn procession, while in a vast dining hall five hundred silent itinerants received their frugal meal from their silent hosts. Over all lingered the recent memory of that vivid throng of gaily dressed pilgrims—transient and ephemeral wraiths—bearing sticks of smoldering incense and flitting like butterflies before their inscrutable gods of wood. Gautama, the "Light of Asia," returning to stand there (even as Confucius before his great temple in Nanking), must surely have felt its charm! Yet if the Sakyamuni were to see how his simple beliefs have been warped and twisted in the course of twenty-four centuries, he would surely feel a very poignant sorrow. The Buddhism of Gautama, based, as it was, upon the "four noble truths"; the broad ethics of Confucius; Taoism, sprung from the pan-theistic principles of Laoutze— all these have sunk to a level of mechanical formalism where their founders could now only very sorrowfully recognize them.

It is a true but sad observation on human affairs that the original greatness of an idea seems always to become limited and bound as it passes from the hands of the few into the hands of the many. Christianity, firmly based upon service and love, has suffered somewhat less than other religions, but we may only feel humility over that. (For what man of us will say that he fully understands the simple, creedless teachings of the Master?) A religion, like a civilization, is, after all, the result of a few great basic ideas. It is not the fault of the teachers, I thought, that we have divided and subdivided those ideas, until, like the fields of the Chinese farmer, there is more soil taken up by useless paths than by growing things.

But if, as the centuries travel on, we can only keep on trying to cut away the useless boundaries of our own small fields—and look up, . . . Why, *then,* perhaps. . . .

CHAPTER VIII

1

ON the highest crag of the island, in a natural rocky hollow quite invisible from below, stood another great yellow-roofed monastery which in prerevolutionary days had been the property of the emperors. It was good to look on, but to reach it, one needed the fitness and determination of a mountain goat. The summit was accessible only by a rugged, rock-hewn stairway of fourteen hundred and fifty steps—a climb which tended to give the handful of superdevout souls who attempted to walk it the certainty (particularly in the legs) that they must be very, very close to heaven.

The majority of lay pilgrims, fresh from bank or shop or office, did not try to climb. They piously purchased cloth-soled sandals— which are the correct footgear for Buddhist pilgrimages in China—and then rode up and down the hill in sedan chairs carried by two straining chair-coolies! The fact that these coolies, who lived on vegetables only, could carry a bamboo chair containing a two-hun-

THE ISLAND OF BUDDHA 145

dred-pound pilgrim up that mighty stairway on the hottest day of August was a shouting victory for vegetarian food—for chair-coolies. But to one who was accustomed neither to vegetable diet nor to such a stupendous flight of steps, the result was not so happy. Long before I reached the hill's crest, the bean curd, bamboo shoots and seaweed soup which had been the daily ration at the Temple of the Grotto, protested bitterly against the calories and vitamines demanded of them. Halfway to the summit was a small pavilion kept by a grave but courtly friar, where those who walked might stop and receive gift-tea. One inscription among the many scribbled on the white walls was in Roman characters. I read it, thinking that it would be one of those quaint and charming monographs on the sea or the sky or some other phase of nature which appear so frequently upon the walls of Chinese temples and pagodas. Instead, it was a short and excellent commentary on the length of the hill.

"C. Wu," it said, "and T. Y. San stop here two time for one drink." Once, without doubt, on the way up, and once on the way down.

At last the cloud-enveloped top of the rock

appeared. The path turned down into a walled courtyard, and again came the glint of imperial yellow. Then—on that small island fifty miles from the China coast, and a thousand feet above the sea—I found myself in the busiest and most prosperous temple that I had seen in China. The outer courts were fairly overwhelmed with waiting chair-coolies who ate melons, cracked pumpkin seeds, called to one another, and romped about unrebuked. The blind poet of Cumæ may never have heard of Cathay, but here was his "resounding portico" with a vengeance! The inner court swarmed with pilgrims of both sexes, who hurried here and there with offerings of cash or bundles of incense, laughing, talking, stopping a moment solemnly to bow before this lacquered god or that and, on the whole, enjoying themselves immensely. Small trousered girls, daughters of the pilgrims proper, dashed about like swift fireflies, leaving a trail of sandalwood smoke behind them. In stepping back to avoid a bevy of these who were bearing down upon a near-by god, I had the great misfortune slightly to bump a very stout lady pilgrim who at the moment was making that profound obeisance, known as the kow-tow, on a little stool, thereby causing her to slip gently off onto the floor where she stood "on all fours" staring at me. I hastened to her aid, but she waved me aside, arose, and turning her back to the sandalwood gods, addressed me with a fluency and vigor that would have done credit to Xantippe herself. While I did not know the actual meaning of the words, it was quite plain that this was not a shower of "blessings and eternal praise." After musing it a few moments in her antique tongue, I called Ah Chow.

"What is the lady saying?" I asked.

"She say," he answered, "if foreign fella stay home, maybe somebody never fall off topside stool."

"Tell the lady," I said, "that I am very sorry indeed."

So he smiled and spoke again in Chinese. But instead of being soothed thereby, she fairly bristled with copper-colored rage, and turning around, called upon Siva, Mi La, and all other available gods to strike the foreigner pink, or words to that general effect. A dowager, evidently, of the school of 1900!

This episode put something of a damper on my visit, therefore after the customary hot towel for my hands (but not my face), I drank the necessary cup of tea and started down the hill meditating on the words of Confucius when he said, "Of all people, women are the most difficult." Suddenly a black suspicion crossed my mind, and I turned to Ah Chow trudging on behind.

"Tell me true words," I said. "What thing you say to that lady?" His wrinkles deepened into an affable smile.

"Oh," he said, "lady make you too much talking. I say, she big damn fool!"

I looked helplessly at that beaming, loyal face. There was nothing to do about it—but at last I understood!

2

The highways of the island were uniformly lined with rows of itinerant friars begging for money to carry them to distant shrines upon the mainland; but in the byways numbers of the younger element were engaged in animatedly passing the time of day by throwing dice, thus proving their kinship to some of Chaucer's gentlemen. There were others of more Anthonian fiber who passed along the roads between the temples carrying small stools over which they would bend at short intervals, bumping their heads sharply against the wooden seats. At last, through constant repetition, the skin of the forehead would break and the blood trickle down over their cheeks. Most of the many thousand itinerants, however, preferred merely to sit by the roadside and receive the welcome alms on their fans or in their laps from the never-ending stream of pilgrims passing by.

Neither beggars nor mendicant monks seemed to expect a gift of more than a cash or two. (There are about twelve cash in a copper cent, varying somewhat with the rate of exchange.) Hence a pilgrim might start out in the morning armed with two dollars' worth of cash—which would weigh about ten pounds—and return at night, weary but content, having distributed a cash apiece to 2,400 Buddhist priests! But, unfortunately, all is not gold that glitters. The grandiose manner in which some of the pilgrims—and alas! the pilgrimesses too—distributed their twelfths-of-a-cent, would, I felt sure, have made their chances for future felicity in the eyes of a discriminating god even less excellent than before—unless perhaps, their own particular bright deity had abandoned the idea of quality in favor of quantity.

At the very edge of the cliff above the sea was a small one-man temple where I frequently enjoyed a *demi-tasse* (of tea) with its merry friar, a brisk, jolly fellow who looked enough like Mi La to have been his brother. He lived all alone and did all the work connected with the temple himself. The place was immaculate. One could drop in at any hour of the day or night and find his house eminently in order. The shrine, the little gods, the garden—all were models of cleanliness. The very bricks of the floor had been polished by hand to so high a mahogany finish that it seemed almost a sacrilege to walk on them. I quite involuntarily won the lasting regard of the little man by leaning down, rubbing the floor with my hand, and then holding it up for him to see that there was not a trace of dust on it. He fairly scintillated with pleasure and padded away at once to get tea, for which he refused any payment whatever. Later, with great pride, he showed me the kitchen, the inner court, and the storeroom. It was as clean as the cleanest house in that land of immaculate houses around the Zuider Zee, and I told him so.

"Perhaps the foreigner would like to buy it," he said, laughing so that his rotund stomach shook with mirth under his gray robe.

"Tell him," I said, "that I live 35,000 *li* away. But I'll take his temple with me anyway."

So, for a few evenings at sunset, I sketched it with the pines and the sea back of it, and the early moon shining across wet sands.

3

Up to that time I had thought that Ah Chow was quite free from superstitions; but one morning he said to me, "I thought-so, you hear devil last night?"

"No—did you?"

"Yessir, last night, I hear man devil. He go past outside my window many time. He say, 'Aw—aw—aw!' very high voice."

"How do you know it wasn't a woman devil?"

"Oh, have got different voice. Man devil say, 'Aw—aw—aw!' Woman devil say 'Ss—ss—ss!' Chinese devil very small. One foot three inch high. No got leg. No can walk. Blow around like one piece paper. If somebody say, 'I hear devil,' must get sick. If somebody say, 'I see devil,' must die. Last night, *I hear devil!*"

With such a self-pronounced Nemesis busily at work among his complexes, it was not strange that by noon he had developed a severe headache. On returning from a walk along the cliffs I found him laid out on his bed with an unknown, begoggled personage bending over him, and half a dozen little lights, like small Christmas candles, sticking out of his face! It looked like a wake! At first sight I feared that he had made an error in his forecasting and had not only heard a devil but seen one as well. A closer inspection, however, showed him to be looking out at me quite calmly from under his illuminations.

"What's all this?" I asked.

"Headache make go way. Take needle cure," he said peacefully; upon which I composed myself and examined his decorations.

Two firmly planted needles were sticking out of each temple, two were solidly imbedded in the middle of his forehead, and three more were sticking out of each eyebrow. On the protruding end of each needle was fastened a small wad of inflammable lint which had been lighted and was blazing merrily away, giving the affair somewhat the color of one of Caligula's evenings "at home," or a Sioux Indian's idea of entertaining a captive. After the needles had become *red hot* and were actually sizzling, they were withdrawn one by one with a pair of tweezers deftly wielded by the stranger, who on receiving thirty-five cents for his (and Ah Chow's) pains, departed to administer his counter-irritant elsewhere.

"How do you feel?" I asked the patient.

"Pretty soon I think maybe can feel pretty good," he answered hopefully. That night I gave him some soda and ten grains of quinine, and by morning the needles had worked a complete cure!

4

The abbot of the Temple of the Grotto wore summer raiment which, for brevity, quite outclassed anything attempted in that direction by Napoleon of the houseboat; for it consisted of a pair of short trunks, a pair of slippers, and a fan. Having reached the age of sixty-two the previous spring, he had retired, leaving the active duties connected with the temple to the old soldier and the others. When the weather was fine he spent the afternoon and half the night in a comfortable wicker chair in the courtyard, smoking his water pipe and looking at the sky. On finding that I was no more fond of going to bed early when the nights were fine than himself, he produced another comfortable wicker chair and invited me to share the moonlight and his water pipe with him. So quite frequently during the calm, Oriental nights that followed we sat there in the temple court—a half-naked Buddhist priest on one side, an American on the other, and a Chinese "boy" squatting in the shadows of the doorway, ready to do the translating that would be necessary. From the great monasteries in the valley off to the right sounded the hollow, distant drumming of the mo-yee and the lift and fall of priests' voices chanting their age-long adaptations of the Brahman Rig-veda, to Quan Yin, the Buddhist Goddess of Mercy. "This," I thought on one such shining occasion, with a thrill of pleasure tingling up and down my spine, "is exactly the sort of thing that one reads about in stories of the East!" My mind was full of questions I should presently ask. The religions of China seemed so hopelessly mixed! In the great temple down the hill, Confucius sat opposite to the god Weito before the shrine of Buddha. La-

THE ISLAND OF BUDDHA

outze, founder of Taoism, was relegated to an inferior place in his own temples and enshrined with two other gods who had been borrowed from Buddhism, yet the Taoist principle that every individual has three souls had permeated both Buddhism and Confucianism!

At that moment the abbot removed the bubbling water pipe from his lips and began to speak. I leaned forward in the wicker chair listening intently to the rhythmic syllables that followed each other in dignified progression from the lips of the venerable man. These might be truths of the deepest theosophic meaning! I might be trembling on the verge of some profound Buddhist mystery! The voice ceased.

"What," I asked, in as even a tone as possible, "what did the Chee Foo say?"

"He say," answered Ah Chow, "this year, potato crop very good."

I smiled; but I was not smiling at the old abbot, who had refilled the tiny bowl of his pipe and was again smoking placidly in the moonlight. I was smiling at an American who, after four intimate months among the everyday Chinese, was still looking for strangeness and complexity where there was so much more of genuineness and simplicity. After that I abandoned the intricacies of Chinese religion and asked the abbot about the island.

Puto-shan, he said, had first become sacred to Buddhism when a wandering monk from India found shelter in a cave on the seaside almost a thousand years ago, during the time of the Later Tang Dynasty. Although the temples were dedicated to Quan Yin, the idealization of Chinese womanhood, no woman lived upon the island. Shrines, temples and monasteries were kept in repair by pilgrims from the mainland who frequently gave large sums of money toward new roofs, intricate carvings, and embroidered hangings. The names of the donors, from emperors to barbers, were to be seen engraved on panels hanging in the various temples.

It was formerly the custom of the imperial rulers of China to visit the island twice every year; and in ancient Sung time, the Emperor Tai-tsing, who was childless, had promised the joss-men of the great, yellow-topped temple in the valley that if only he might have a son, he would dedicate him to the service of their temple. In course of time the gracious and compassionate lady, Quan Yin, sent a son to the

THE ISLAND OF BUDDHA

royal household. The joss-men immediately reminded the emperor of his promise, but now that a child had really arrived, the imperial parent was no longer sanguine about parting with him. After all, the Dynasty was the thing! So commanding his artists and silversmiths, he caused them to carve out of silver a life-size image of the boy, which he sent with greetings to the temple. The priests, who were by that time beginning to be a little worried at their forceful demand, and who were thinking that, after all, an emperor's son might be something of a white elephant on their hands, accepted the gift with great satisfaction. To this day it stands well guarded in the house of the high priest on the hillside back of the temple.

"Is it possible to see the statue?" I asked the Chee Foo. The old man sat up in the moonlight, blew the ashes out of his water pipe, and smiled.

"If you will shave off your hair, burn the twelve sacred spots on your head, and become a Buddhist priest, you can see it very easily," he said.

Well—so much for that! But it is hardly necessary to say that when I left Puto-shan two days later I had not seen the silver statue.

THE LITTLE HOUSE

CHAPTER IX

1

ABOVE all other possible Chinese experiences was one in particular which cried aloud for fulfillment. I had not yet lived with a Chinese family. Whether it could be managed was somewhat doubtful; native living places were not advertised in the Shanghai Chinese press. The likeliest way of finding a room, it seemed, was to make a house-to-house search for certain small, red squares of paper pasted beside the house doors, which, Ah Chow informed me, announced that there was a room to rent. On our room-hunting expeditions through the byways of Shanghai I usually went on ahead and pointed out each red square of paper to Ah Chow. Then Ah Chow would amble up in his near-sighted way, and, standing there with his blue cotton gown hanging straight from his drooping shoulders, and the old black fedora, of which he was so proud, pulled down over his wrinkled-up face, he would slowly unravel the meaning of the beautiful, brush-drawn marks on the placard before him. Sometimes the characters did not mean "Room for rent" at all, but told that the householder had given a sum of money to a benevolent lottery, or that certain Japanese pills were good pills, or that a member of the family had run away and a reward was offered for his or her—generally her—return. Sometimes the family doctor was expected, and then a blank square of paper was pasted to the wall to direct him to the right house.

But often enough to make it interesting, there came a poster announcing a vacant room. Then Ah Chow would straighten his old back, swallow hard, assume a jaunty, jovial manner and plunge in as though he expected nothing but success. After he had explained his mission, I would be presented; but in spite of the fact that Ah Chow had already told the good people that the room was wanted by a foreigner, the shock of actually seeing such a person right in their own domain was far too great, and they only recovered themselves just in time to say that they wanted a lady roomer (Chinese), or a married couple (Chinese), or a Sikh policeman or anything else that popped into their heads.

"Must can find pretty soon," Ah Chow

would say hopefully; and then there was nothing for it but to smile and go on to the next place. On the fifth day of the search a leading editorial came out in the largest Chinese daily paper warning its readers against taking nondescript foreigners into their homes. Such foreigners, the editorial said, were often trying to hide from the police! That was somewhat discouraging, but we kept on looking. Perhaps there would be a small house on a side street somewhere, anywhere. . . .

2

At last we found it. A round-arched gateway disclosed a short, high-walled lane which had four doorways on each side, and ended in a blank wall. Except for a few children and ducks and chickens, the lane was quite empty; and it was clean. A vermilion patch of paper on the gateway said that a room in the third house on the left-hand side was for rent. I looked at the cleanness of the place, and I knew that I was weary. If it pleased the household gods, I would stop right there.

"Ah Chow," I said, "if can stay this house, I give you five dollars."

We knocked and entered. A young man, a

young woman and an old woman who were busily plying their chopsticks at a table in the court, stopped and greeted us, while Ah Chow launched briskly into the matter in hand. Whether by virtue of an extra eloquence on Ah Chow's part, the brightness of the October day, the satisfactory contents of the rice bowls, or a combination of all three, it soon became agreeably apparent that a foreigner as tenant was not objectionable. The room for rent was upstairs; so following the young man (whose name was Hop Lee) we went up the shaky, ladderlike steps at the back of the house to the second story. Here, as on the ground floor, were two narrow rooms with a passage along the side which made the vacant back room only eight feet square. That was very small if there were to be palettes and wet canvases about, and besides, the kitchen was in a little lean-to on the ground just below; and I had already been sufficiently smoked at Anking. How about the front room?

The front room, Hop Lee said, had been occupied for five years by a gentleman who smoked opium—but he would see. After some discussion the matter was arranged. The opium gentleman, who probably felt that he had a potent enough smoke of his own to combat any that might arise from the kitchen, was quite willing, for a slight consideration, to take the back room. So Ah Chow, returning to the Oriental Hotel, which had again afforded temporary shelter, hired two wheelbarrow men and came rumbling back over Soochow Creek.

The little lane was so secluded that the crowd which gathered in front of the door consisted only of the immediate neighbors. The coming of a foreigner seemed to be a very solemn occasion—almost sober enough to call forth whispers. So I smiled at some of the little boys who stood nearby; whereupon the affair so thoroughly shed its funereal aspect that a native policeman strolled into the lane to see what the racket was about.

The house itself was a narrow, two-story building, built solidly in a block with those on either side. The street gate led into a small, inclosed court in a corner of which was a lacquered stand holding three tiers of flowering plants. A living room back of the court contained tables and chairs placed squarely against the walls, a portrait of a deceased ancestor above a small pewter shrine opposite the entrance, and a motto in black, brush-drawn characters on an orange scroll against each side wall. Back of the living room was the bedroom of Hop Lee, his young wife, his wife's mother, and his small daughter. During the day the old grandmother sat in the sunlit court crooning a never-changing melody to the mystic words, *"O mi do vah."* Whenever I passed she would stop her song and address certain agreeable remarks to me in her own tongue, and I would agreeably answer in mine; and then, as each emphatically agreed with the spirit, at least, of what the other had said, we would both go on about our business. Hop Lee himself, a pleasant young fellow of affable manner, was an entertainer at banquets, weddings, and similar functions—a sort of troubadour who not only had an endless répertoire of songs and ballads, but who played with vigor and precision on the flute, the moon guitar, and the Chinese violin. His young wife, left to her own devices for a great part of the time, seemed to suffer from considerable boredom, which, however, would have been much worse had it not been for a never-ending game of neighborhood dominoes, the click and clatter of which could be heard at any hour of the day or night.

But the Orient pearl of the household was the wee daughter, Dah Zon. Diminutive white trousers, cut like those of a Persian princess, swept to her ankles. The waistband, fastened well up under her arms, gave her plump, rotund little body and chubby bare shoulders an effect indescribably bewitching. Upon her feet were small red shoes embroidered with colored silks. Her somewhat oval face with its fresh lips, rosy cheeks, and large brown eyes, was punctuated with ever-so-slightly tipped-up eyebrows and two shiny little black braids, one of which appeared at each side tied with a bunch of red cord. But the crowning glory was another small Brownie-like tentacle of hair rising straight up from the top of her head where it nodded and bobbed with every emotion. At sight of her, Moloch himself must, for the time, have forgotten all thoughts of frightfulness and allowed her to make nests in his primeval beard. When she spoke, it was the young Scheherazade lisping her first immaculate, silvery version of the *Arabian Nights*. To put it still more frankly, I admitted to love at first sight.

The winning of a Chinese lady, aged five, however, is not a thing to be accomplished in any crude Lochinvar manner. I brought her a large red apple, but she only drew back, took refuge behind her thumb, and looked hard at me. Too hard, in fact. There was obviously something the matter with my face. It was so *different!* I tried to obliterate myself in a sort of patrol formation—apple first as the "point," then myself as the "main body"—but out came the thumb, the lips began to quiver, and only by a quickly maneuvered retreat up the rickety stair was I spared the ignominy of tear-shed. After that, I passed her, not proudly but with averted head until the day when she should become better accustomed to my presence, and— *Deo favente*—to my face.

3

All painting had up to that time been restricted mainly to the Chinese landscape. True, I had painted the innkeeper at Anking; and on the Grand Canal I had attempted a sketch of a boy sleeping in a boat, but I had been set upon by his parents with such threatening, agonized gestures and entreaties that I had scraped it down with a palette knife, and on returning to the houseboat had immediately inquired how I had offended the Chinese pro-

THE LITTLE HOUSE

prieties. Chinese people, it seemed, were painted only after they were dead, and even then only by proxy. The relatives of the dead would go to the shop of a professional portrait painter who had among his properties a hundred or more photographs, half-tones, and woodcuts of different types of Chinese faces. There they would select the picture that looked most like the departed, the portrait painter would make a large painting of the same, clothe it in regal robes of paint and send it to the family, who would hang it up (as in the house of Hop Lee) beside the family shrine. Therefore, to have one's picture painted while one was still alive would give gods and men the very erroneous impression that one was already dead! One might quite as well *be* dead as to allow that!

But the house of Hop Lee seemed to be a better base from which to work than the houseboat had been. I resolved to try it again. Two things were necessary: first, a place in which to paint, and second, models. The first was easily arranged. On the main street a few doors from the lane stood a large group of old buildings behind high walls. This had once been a Confucian temple, but was now owned by a certain philanthropic organization of a neighboring city which took care of all of its fellow townsmen who died in Shanghai, and transported the dead in thick coffins to their native city. Permission was obtained to use a small open court between two of the buildings, isolated and silent except for the noise of the coffin makers in an adjoining shed. So much for the studio.

When it came to getting models, even the usually resourceful Ah Chow was out of ideas and admitted it. Among his large and varied Shanghai acquaintance he could find no one who was willing to sacrifice the good luck of a lifetime for two dimes, or even three, an hour. The only manner of procedure seemed to be to walk along the street until someone of suitable type appeared, and then stop and inquire into the possibilities of the situation. But the answer was always in the negative. To have one's picture painted was bad enough. To have it painted by a foreigner was worse; but to have it painted by a foreigner in a coffin yard—well—one might just as well go over to Soochow Creek and jump right off the bridge! "We will have our pictures painted *after* we are dead," they said, emphatically.

The outlook was discouraging. But when every possible plan seemed to have been exhausted, Ah Chow came to me and said, "You like to find model fella, make paint him?" As that had been the object of every waking moment for several days, I replied a little curtly that I would. Ah Chow's face took on a strange, woodenish expression.

"Can find plenty any time," he said in the most bland and suave manner imaginable!

"Well then why in ——!" Steady, Anglo-Saxon! Steady! This good fellow has been working with great intelligence for you for months, and it is probable that his intentions are still most excellent. The truth is, he has just at this minute thought of some plan or other to get models and is telling you about it at once. But he is ashamed not to have thought of the scheme before and so he is playing that little old Oriental game called "saving the face." "Where can you find models?" I asked.

"Must go see loafer fella in tea shop," he said. "One loafer fella have got one street. He big boss on his street. He know all robber, beggar, tief. Somebody steal something in Shanghai, loafer fella can find in three hours."

"And you think you can find a model at his tea shop?"

"Oh, yesser!" came the enthusiastic answer, "he doan care—foreigner, devil, anything!" And with those winged words, he departed for the tea shop in question, returning in the course of an hour not with a "loafer fella" but with a sort of henchman—a composite-looking little man of fifty, thin as a clothes-horse and wearing a beard consisting of not more than twenty-five long black hairs. After holding his pose for the first half hour, he decided that the risk was too great, and left precipitately. The next model was a beggar whose knee joints were so stiff that he could pose only standing up; but his face was typically Chinese, and he held his position like a man of iron. As it became noised abroad that ill-luck did not immediately follow employment in the coffin-yard, models became easier to find, but they were always beggars—probably because they had so little to lose.

4

In the little house on Wai-on-fon Lane—for that was the lane's name—one could very easily follow Pasteur Wagner in leading the simple life. There was not room enough to be

Blind beggars frequently travel about in groups—a most touching sight. These are in Shanghai.

complex. The house was only twelve feet wide, and the length of it from front to back was not more than twenty-two feet. In my own room the effect of a compact interior was heightened by Ah Chow, who, fearing to leave provisions in the general kitchen in the lean-to, used the unoccupied corners for baskets of bamboo shoots, bean sprouts, and other useful flora. One night when I came home in the dark, my face unexpectedly brushed against some unknown, hair-raising substance in mid-air—which turned out to be a string of blushing Canton sausages suspended from a hook on my improvised hatrack.

Peace seemed to have found a permanent abiding place in the little house. The young musician and his wife never quarreled, the old grandmother sang her daily songs, and Dah Zon, playing in the lane, received no more than the occasional bumps and scratches which are necessary to a successful childhood. The opium gentleman in the next room was a short, bald-headed man of fifty, who for thirty years had been smoking Indian opium. In spite of his dignified manner and healthy appearance, it was plain that every energy, every interest was centered in his drug. He procured, prepared, and smoked his daily *mace* with a calm but terrible concentration. Everything else was blotted out.

The window blinds in my room extended only half way up the windows. Occasionally, after taking "'setting-up" exercises in the morning, I would throw open the blinds just in time to see half a dozen heads disappearing from the windows across the lane where the householders had been absorbed in watching the strange appearance and disappearance of hands and arms above my blinds. But even the complexities of "setting-up" exercises ceased when Ah Chow, who had long since become inured to the peculiar customs of a foreigner, appeared one morning with his usually sober face wrinkled into deep lines of mirth and said, "Old lady in next house say, 'Foreign man must be very good. He pray so hard he shake down plaster and break one cup!'"

During one of the early morning walks with which I replaced the morning gymnastics, I saw a small toy dog in a Japanese shop. At that time there was more or less of an embargo on Japanese goods, all through the Yangtze valley; nevertheless, the dog in question seemed to be the perfect token of regard for the young Chinese lady who looked upon me so coldly. The canine's cloth hide was tan, his eyes were shoe buttons, and his legs were built solidly and far apart like the pillars of a German rathskeller. The fact that one had to hit him sharply on the head to make him bark seemed to neutralize any prejudice which might have been connected with his nationality. The presentation was a success, but on mounting to my chamber, I almost immediately heard cries of despair from below. Ah Chow, the faithful courier, brought the tidings.

"Have broke already," he said.

"How can break?" I asked; "dog no have got something to break!"

"Have break *noise!*" said Ah Chow. "Hit him on head plenty time. Pretty soon, dog never say something!"

Unfortunate—very! But I resolved that the friendly intentions of America toward China should not suffer from any further foreign complication. The next present was to be strictly Chinese.

5

The episode of the dog was followed by a

decided coolness. The mere fact that one gave presents that would break, was *not* a matter of credit. But in the course of time I purchased a duck, a handsome lacquered duck of solid wood which I placed before the royal footstool and went my way.

To all who would win the affections of a Chinese lady not over six years I recommend a wooden duck. For as I sat reading that old stoic, Epictetus (whom I found to be a great aid after Chinese meals), the sprite Scheherazade herself appeared in my doorway, half-clad as usual, with a smile dimpling her small oval face. It was evident that the duck which she held tightly in her hand had settled the matter of friendship once for all, for she came right in without the slightest diffidence and made herself entirely at home. Epictetus, in spite of his red leather binding and gold lettering, did not hold her long, so I showed her some views of Shanghai. She looked at them without concern. An electric flashlight did somewhat better, and she played with it for several minutes while I was casting about for the next means of entertainment. When the flashlight (as well as its battery) was exhausted, I exhibited some photographs of places along the Yangtze.

But only one—that of a Chinese mother and her young family—attracted her attention, and in her light, silvery tongue, she babbled something or other about *ny-ang,* which is the Chinese word for "mother."

She next examined in quick succession a picture of the poacher Shakespeare, before Sir Thomas Lucy, a silver cigarette case, a safety razor (sans blade), and a pair of shell-rimmed spectacles; but these matters left her unimpressed, and she descended abruptly from her chair to see what she could see by herself.

6

In one corner of the room stood a large, unfinished painting of three coolies squatting in the temple yard playing *hwo-jun,* that universal game of chance which the Italians play under the name of *morra.* The paint was very wet. I ought to have known that there was trouble ahead—but I didn't.

Scheherazade tripped lightly toward the painting and stood contemplating it in that position so dear to art critics—hands clasped behind, head thrown back, feet slightly astride as though to balance body and judgment at the same time.

"This," I thought, "will be the most naïve art criticism I have ever had." Were the characteristics of the coolies clear enough for her to recognize them? Would she give vent to some expression of feeling which showed that she knew them as beings familiar to her own experience?

She would, and did! With one swift, concentrated swipe of her small pink hand she wrecked the faces of those coolies so that their dearest friends would not have known them. And then (shades of Argive Helen and all the rest!) after the havoc she wrought, she held out that same diminutive hand to me to be washed! So, grinning joyfully like any other fool-there-was, I got out the turpentine and soap and washed it clean as snow—and the other hand as well. But the wooden duck would no longer have been a covenant between us if she had known the words of Mr. Kipling which were on my lips—words about the years we waste and the tears we waste—as I carried her downstairs to her maternal ancestor.

CHAPTER X

1

SPOKEN English rests firmly on the great submerged base of the East-Midland dialect. Spoken Chinese rests firmly on nothing at all. The written characters, it is true, are identical everywhere in China proper; but the pronunciation is so varied that the vast country is linguistically broken up into a dozen or more distinct language areas, each shading into each other through numberless dialects. Peking, Shanghai, and Canton are separated from one another approximately as are New York, Chicago, and Santa Fe. But the citizens of the three Chinese cities speak languages which differ from each other almost as much as French from English or English from German. For example, a common friction match is a *yong-chu-sze* in Peking, a *sze-lai-hwo* in Shanghai, and a *foo-chai* in Canton. At Nanking, less than two hundred miles from Shanghai, it is not a *sze-lai-hwo* but a *yong-hwo*.

With such varied changes in dialect, it was difficult, during a short stay in any one place, to advance much further than simple greetings and remarks about the weather. But Ah Chow's gallant skirmishes with English more than recompensed for my incapacity in Chinese. Strangely enough, he had little difficulty with the *r* which usually gives the Chinese so much trouble. *Fruit pie,* indeed, was always aerated into a more windy delicacy, *flute pie; very* under excitement became *velley,* and *rice* was—also mispronounced; but that was all. Occasionally, like Francis Thompson, he strayed into the realm of etymological invention and coined a shining new word from two old ones. *Clever* and *careful* were joined into *clayful;* suitor and sweetheart became *swaytor;* while *jetty,* where the baggage was examined, and *duty,* which was often exacted at the jetty by the customs officials, were wedded into *jootey.*

But these things were only stepping-stones to higher planes of conquest. Sometimes, during our conversations on matters of Chinese usage and behavior, he would look solemnly at me out of his good eye and give utterance to a maxim that would rise up as upon a wingéd horse and roost gallantly on the very citadel of modern verse. Here are a few selected at random:

THE LITTLE HOUSE

Have Got
Have got three younger brothers.
Just now
Get along pretty good;
Before, sometimes must take meat-chopper,
Sometimes, small hatchet.

Young Lady
Evening, very good looking;
Morning, like devil.

Proper Man
Proper man
Live in one house
A long-long time

. . . .

I live in my house
Fourteen years.

Woman
Woman,
Very trouble.

Babies
More small,
More naughty.

2

Some time before coming to the little house I had sadly abandoned the use of chopsticks. The unsurmountable obstacle was—rice. The accepted Chinese way of eating rice was not to take up a few grains at a time with the chopsticks—an endless task—but to place the rice bowl to the lips and by using the sticks from the side with a rotary motion, get the rice at all hazards into the mouth. Anyone who has eaten his meals from the narrow panel of a one-armed chair in an American "dairy lunch" knows with what prodigious speed a piece of apple or even mince pie can disappear. But the pie-eating motion is not a rotary motion, it is a piston motion. There is something inherent in the Anglo-Saxon nature which rebels at placing a bowl to the lips and shovelling—an inhibition not so strongly marked in the spaghetti-eating Latin races who seem to react to still another series of complexes. (Along with the Chinese *manu forte* technique of eating rice is a *bel canto* method of sipping tea, which, if properly learned, has the most sustained tone in the world. A coolie who can not be heard sipping tea at fifty yards is probably a sick man and needs tending to.) Such sounds from the nearby restaurants came only faintly to the house on Wai-on-fon Lane, for the Lane had plenty of noises of its own. During the day it resounded with the cries and laughter of its children, the barks of its dogs,

THE LITTLE HOUSE 183

and the occasional squeals of wandering pigs; and it may go on record that dogs never howled, pigs never squealed, and babies never roared with more zest and love of life than right below my window. In a small coop in the court next door there were three young roosters, but they hardly lasted beyond their adolescence, for they "sang" at night and so brought down sudden doom upon themselves. It was thought to be a premonition of bad luck for roosters to "sing" at night. It was at least bad luck for the roosters.

The dogs of the lane, following established dog-etiquette, slept exactly in the middle of the thoroughfare. When stepped on, they would awaken, howl with every ounce of energy they could muster, and then go peacefully to sleep in the identical spot from which they had been aroused. Each dog knew his own sector down to the fraction of an inch, and it went badly with any smaller dog who infringed on his territory. But unless sleep is a vice they could hardly have been called vicious. Usually in the cities along the Yangtze, instead of taking a ricksha, I had preferred to walk; yet in many miles of narrow, crowded streets, I was never snapped at by a dog, and I never saw a dog snap at anyone else. They would bark, it is true, as I came along, and sometimes pass the word that a foreigner was approaching, to the dogs for half a mile ahead until the promenade sounded like feeding-time at a canine menagerie. But their attitude was only one of embarrassment quite free from all trace of bitterness. They felt much worse about it than I did . . .

At frequent intervals during the day, slow-moving venders with baskets of cakes, fruits, flowers, or vegetables would sound their individual street cries or make their own particular noises on bamboo or gongs while merchants, two by two, carrying between them large boxes filled with calico, stopped between the houses and began a lusty, syncopated harangue about the high quality of their goods. Then the little, smooth-haired housewives, modestly dressed in high-necked pajamas, would patter out to see whether true words were being spoken. Soon their voices, clear as the music of a dozen xylophones, would rise in staccato syllables of protest. Most of the time, true words, it appeared, were *not* being spoken.

On the whole sketching in the coffin-yard

progressed very smoothly. There were never more than twenty spectators at a time standing about the sketching-easel, a condition which, after the vast crowds I had been buried in along the canals in the earlier houseboat days, gave me the feeling of being quite alone. There were always several distinct stages to the making of a sketch as far as the crowd was concerned. When I started, all was silence. Then shortly some feature or detail clear enough to recognize appeared. Some one would boom out the glad tidings, and the rest of the onlookers (already practically sitting in my lap or climbing over my shoulder) would charge en masse, entirely shutting the subject from view—breathing, coughing, and sneezing on me quite unconsciously in their almost spellbound curiosity. I had tried putting the sketching-umbrella down very low over my head, but it did no good. There were always five or six of us under the umbrella together! However, if one were patient, that stage passed too. There were even rare times when for all of three minutes one could paint without a single interruption.

Sometimes when I had been painting from the houseboat, young mothers who had been watching would go into their houses and return again proudly carrying their infant sons. Usually I nodded in the pleasant congratulatory way which they seemed to expect. (Boys were indeed a matter of congratulation, for some day they would be able to take care of their parents if necessary, and they would never be lost to the clan by marriage as girls almost invariably were.) But once in a while—just to see what would happen—I paid no attention at all. And then the young wife, after waiting a few minutes, would toss her head as much as to say, "Stupid thing! Too busy to notice a *boy!*" and disappear permanently. Even in the coffin-yard, each day had its own unexpected fillip or twist. One afternoon, a woman with a speckled-looking baby on her arm came along crying but paused long enough to see what I was doing. Later I asked Ah Chow, who had held the baby, what was the matter.

"Oh," he said, "very trouble. She have got three little children at home with smallpox. *She think baby have got it too!*"

3

Quite often, while the models were rest-

THE LITTLE HOUSE 187

ing, I stopped and watched the coffin-makers at their work. Coffins appeared to play a very important rôle in the life of the people. The nicest, friendliest gift that one could present or receive was a coffin. If a man's friends did not believe in gifts of so practical a nature, he would often buy a coffin himself and keep it in a conspicuous place about the house, showing it with pride to all visitors. That plan seemed a little morbid at first; but, after all, I thought, one would very soon get used to the idea of looking at its solid, nicely finished, six-inch timbers in a friendly way, and thinking, "Well, this is the little house which will some day very snugly hold the mortal part of me." It was conceivable—so I thought as I luxuriated in the fine, broad philosophy of a perfectly healthy man—that one might even pat it a few times and look it over affectionately for any possible cracks! But I had temporarily forgotten one of Mr. Noah Webster's most important definitions about man. A man, he says, is one of the pieces with which certain games, such as chess or draughts, are played.

It was the season of the Fall Festival. With the crisp, invigorating air of early October the city seemed to awaken. Banners flashed in the sunlight, gay decorations sprang up overnight, and the white garments of summer yielded to silken apparel of blue, brown, gray, and green which sang a colorful chorus along the brilliant, sunlit streets. Festivity was rampant. Sounds of rejoicing and the callow voice of the Chinese fiddle were heard everywhere; debts were paid and people gave each other congratulatory boxes of roasted chestnuts and delicious Chinese cakes. In four weeks the steamship *Empress of Asia,* on which I had engaged a passage, was scheduled to sail for home. I abandoned myself to merriment. I ate the Chinese cakes . . .

And then one day when the sun was shining brightest and the colors were gayest, I felt a small pain on my right-hand side just below the belt—a small, trivial pain, but steady; relentlessly steady. At first I refused to be coerced. "Pooh!" I said to the pain, "you're only fooling!" But it stayed. For two weeks I neither enjoyed the gay sunshine nor admired the holiday decorations. I ate poached eggs on toast, and the days were forty-eight hours long. Even painting in the coffin-yard lost its attractive quaintness, and the orderly

THE LITTLE HOUSE 189

rows of nice, shiny, black coffins were passed quite unnoticed—except when I remembered that the notes for this final chapter had been taken down under the title of "The Little House." Why had I called it *that*, I wondered. Of all unpleasant titles for a last chapter—"The Little House"!

Finally, when there was no doubt about it, I went to Dr. Tucker of Saint Luke's Hospital in Shanghai.

"Yes," said Dr. Tucker, "that's the way it looks to me."

. . . .

Two weeks later—at eight thirty-five on the night of October 27th I sat once more in my room in the house of Hop Lee. The moon as of old, rising round and full beyond the Wangpoo, glowed in a perfect orb of splendor over the sweeping, dark-tiled roofs of the city. A Chinese flute in a nearby court tossed showers of crystal sound into the moonlight. The night was Oriental, and it was Chinese.

But something seemed to be wrong. The spell of China, if not irreparably broken, was at least badly bent. Hospital care, white-clad nurses, meals à la française, beds with springs, and the general comforts of the last fortnight had so dispersed the Chinese atmosphere that I no longer contemplated the thought of resting on a bedding-roll (which in turn rested on three wide boards) with perfect Chinese equanimity. Even Scheherazade herself had failed to make the homecoming all that it might have been, by thumping me sharply on the one section of my anatomy least fitted by recent events to receive an embrace. Acrid fumes from the next room drifted in through the wooden partition. The opium gentleman was cooking his drug—three dollars' worth at a time—which lasted two days. The fragrance of opium being smoked is not bad when one gets used to it, but *raw* opium being cooked would never be mistaken for a distillation of violets and asphodel. I rose for air and went to the window, looking at my watch on the table as I went. It was eight thirty-seven. At that moment—quite without warning—an explosion of firecrackers swept over the entire city, roaring and rippling down the main streets and sputtering along the lanes in a seething flood of noise. I looked to the right and to the left and down into the court below. In spite of the quivering atmosphere, everything appeared to be quite as usual. I looked up at the sky—and then I saw what was the matter. Something was happening to the moon! Along its lower edge, a dirty-looking yellowish crescent was slowly extending itself over that foolish, good-natured face. No wonder the firecrackers exploded and the gongs sounded! Every child in China knew the story of what was happening:

> *Ching Cháng O,*
> *Wife of Han,*
> *Stole some pills from her good man,*
> *Pills of everlasting life;*
> *Fled to the moon,*
> *Wicked old wife!*
> *Butza turned her to a toad,*
> *Now she sits the live-long night*
> *On the moon,*
> *Wicked old crone!*
> *Of its light she takes a bite,*
> *Sometimes swallows every bit!*
>
> *Bang the mo-yee, blow the sang,*
> *Pound the lo and make it clang;*
> *If you make a noise, why soon*
> *She will give you back the moon!*

At nine twenty-five, all light was gone from its face, and the moon hung in the sky dull as the under side of a large brown turnip, with a slightly lighter color in the center where the root belonged. Now was the time to blow the mo-yee and pound the sang! Now, if ever, was the time to frighten the toad. Altogether —*Now!* Noise reached its maximum density. The night seemed to resolve itself into a liquid carrying a complete saturation of sound. Neighbors' wives ran out on their verandahs, laughing and holding their ears, dogs barked, babies screamed, boys whistled. Everyone was laughing and excited—everyone except the opium gentleman in the back room. Only death itself would interfere with his terrible calm as he prepared his daily ration of dreams. Suddenly a glad cry sounded from all quarters of the city, for a gleam of light had appeared at the lower edge of the turnip. *The toad was relinquishing her prey!*

With great content I laid me down to sleep under the wide eaves of the house of Hop Lee. What difference did a hard bed make *now?* The spell of China had returned!

6

Indeed, one may now say, "The spell of China *has* returned"—for it was not further away than last night that the eclipse occurred;

THE LITTLE HOUSE

and it is no further away than to-morrow that the *Empress of Asia* will be plowing out through the shallows at the mouth of the Yangtze, toward home. There is just time for one more walk down to the Bund on the waterfront where the ships of a score of nations are lying at anchor.

Saying good-bye to Ah Chow and the little maid, Dah Zon, we leave the lane and very soon reach Soochow Creek, which, spanned by many bridges and swarming with junks and houseboats, lies sparkling in the sunlight. Down the jetty along the water's edge comes a caravan of wheelbarrows. The straining coolies are almost buried under huge canvas bags piled to a height of eight or ten feet on each side of the vehicle's single wheel. A bag gaps a little showing its contents. It is full of white, glistening cocoons. They are being carried from the river junks to the great silk-filature manufactories, where thousands of girls, trained in the most delicate industrial work in the world, unroll, strand by strand, the fragile shrouds of the silk insects. Watching the wheelbarrows, we almost stumble over a woman who is kneeling with bowed head at the edge of the sidewalk. Directly under her face is a wet spot on the sidewalk into which tears are actually dropping from her eyes! I have never seen the beginning of one of those puddles—it must be a highly astonishing process—but I have seen both men and women crying bona fide tears, apparently for hours at a time, into their respective pools to enlist the sympathy of passers-by.

There is a group of sew-sew women sitting on the sidewalk mending clothes. Some of them are wearing inch-wide, circular black patches at their temples to prevent headache—decorations which bring back the memory of some beautiful old woodcuts in a musty copy of *Gulliver's Travels*. But these women are busy with other kinds of patches, and will repair a gaping void in a pair of coolie trousers for two cents. The fact that the patch is blue and the garment black makes no difference to them or to their customers. It is only a hole that is disgraceful! Beside them stands a little boy with four vaccination marks in a row on his arm. His family is taking no unnecessary chances with smallpox; but there is a sore on his arm with something which appears to be a pink plaster over it. Unfortunately, it is not a plaster. It is half of a pink cigarette box on which we can read the gold lettering, "Ruby Queen"!

Half-a-dozen urchins playing along the water front are seen to be wearing each a single earring. That (say it softly) is so the devils will think they are girls, for Chinese girls are not as interesting to devils as boys who will support their parents in old age. These lads are full of animal spirits. It is quite possible that when a foreigner goes past, they may nudge each other and say with much laughter, "There goes your uncle!" But it is only the exuberance of youth; and we must not forget that once when a Chinese ambassador was out for a dignified promenade along the Potomac, one of our own Young Ideas stood on the opposite curbstone and shouted, "Hello, John! You makee washee-washee?"

At a street corner we are halted by a tram which stops with the third-class trailer directly opposite to us. Perhaps you are familiar with the "loop" in Chicago, or the Métropolitain in Paris, or the Interborough in New York at those hours of the day when human beings become smiling savages and rend each other for the privilege of being packed among their fellows like sardines in a tin. Nevertheless, you will stand quite still and watch this Chinese crowd storm the trailer. If Coach Roper of Princeton and "Bob" Fisher of Harvard were here beside us, they would also stand and watch, and they would get a number of new and excellent ideas for next season's football in end-runs and slipping through the line.

Just as the simultaneous diving in and out of the door is at its wildest, the conductor of the trailer blows his whistle to show that personally he is quite ready to go ahead, and the car moves off with a tail of people stringing out behind like a swarm of bees when the queen decides to move. A stout, pleasant-looking citizen and his comely wife and two small children are in the front rank just as the whistle blows. One child, indeed, is already inside the door, and the mother is on the step. Extricating herself, she jumps off before the car gathers speed and runs along beside it, tugging at the hand of the infant inside, who is wedged between the legs of the passengers. The good citizen hurls himself upon the step, separates the tightly clasped hands, pries the child out from among many legs, and jumps backward off of the car, retaining his balance only by a miracle of equilibrium. For an American family to treat itself thus roughly would almost spoil the day. But these people are Chinese—and here comes another car! They seize the other infant, who has been left at the street crossing, and project themselves aboard, breathless but smiling.

7

We continue our walk along the broad thoroughfare beside Soochow Creek. Here at last is the Bund, and here are the Public Gardens with their great trees, well kept lawns and gay flowers. Sitting down on one of the benches, we see the miles of docks, engineering works, cotton mills and shipyards in the distance. On the wide expanse of water between, moves the amazing, ceaseless traffic of the harbor. But I, for one, am thinking about another matter. In the house on the lane, there has been a book in the making, not about mandarins and dignitaries, but about everyday people—boatmen and coolies and dwellers in small houses—and it has tried to show some of the humor and the simplicity and the kindliness which are unfailingly to be found among them. Looking out over the water, I realize with a feeling of mingled regret and relief that the book is finished. Well—it is right enough for it to be finished. One cannot, I think to myself, spend all one's days here on the China coast!

No? Like a keen, alluring challenge from across the harbor, comes the buoyant song of the Chinese boatmen, as they raise their sails on the high-prowed ships which travel by wind from Shanghai down to the sea.

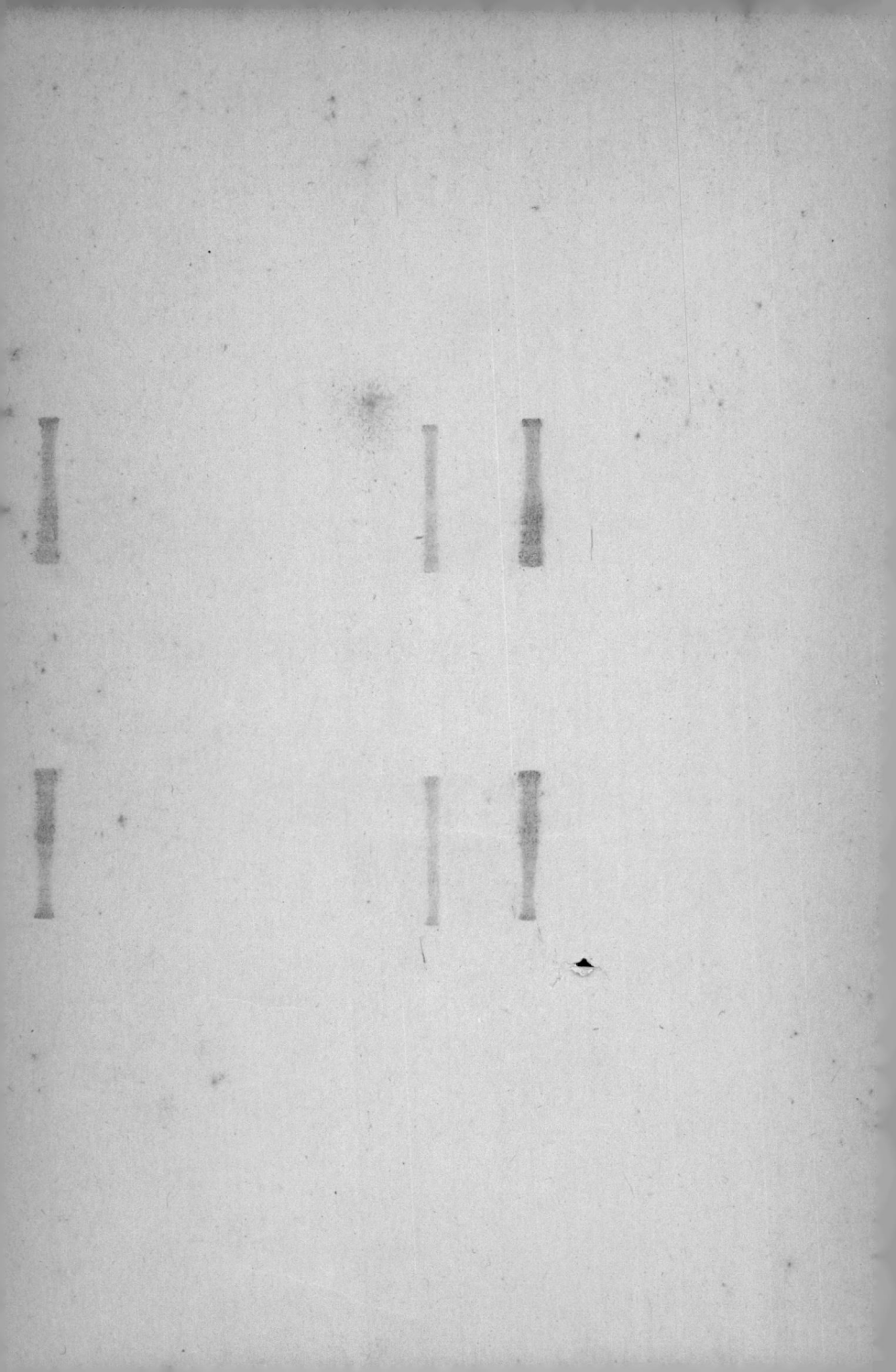